quick curtains

quick curtains

CHRIS JEFFERYS

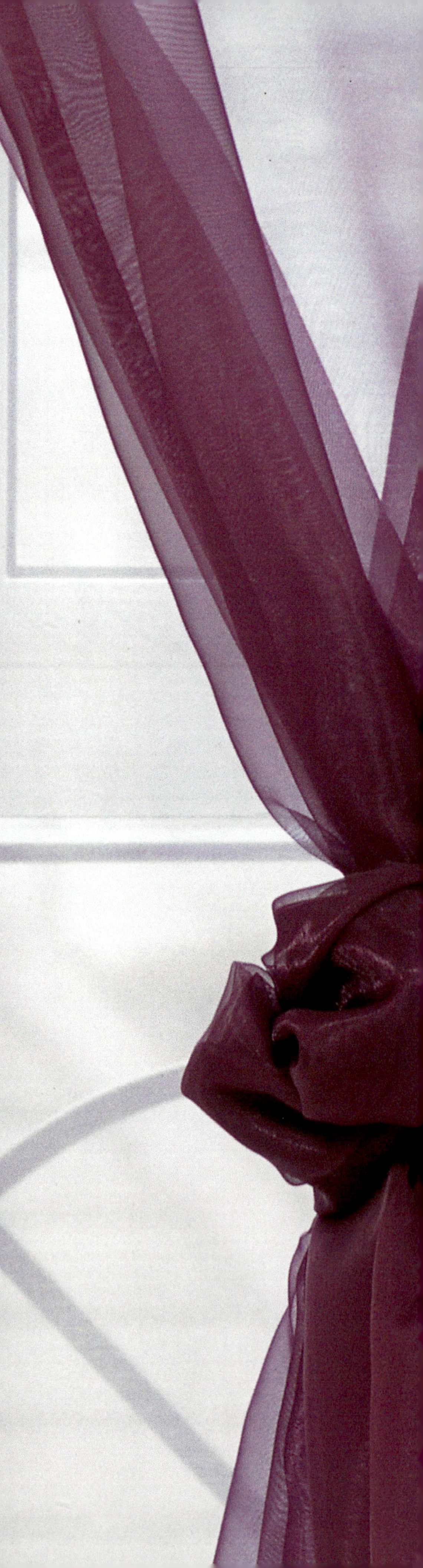

First published in 2006 by New Holland Publishers (UK) Ltd
Senior Editor: Corinne Masciocchi
Illustrator: Coral Mula
Photographer: Shona Wood
Curtain makers: Gwen Diamond, Vicky French and Melanie Williams
Editorial Direction: Rosemary Wilkinson
Production: Hazel Kirkman

ISBN: 978-1-5048-0149-2

Printed in the USA

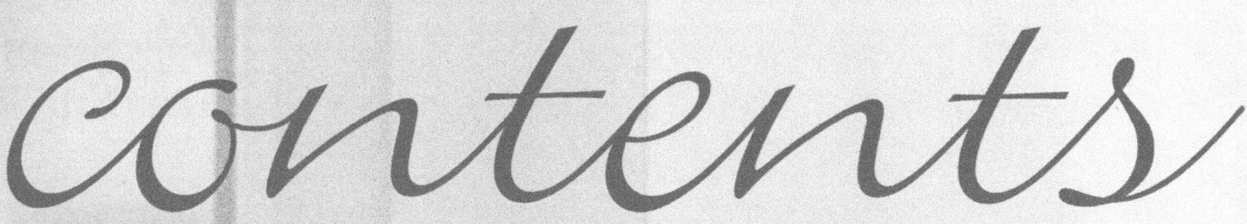

contents

introduction

Curtains are a quick and easy way to change or update the colour scheme of a room. Making curtains need not to be complicated – a smart tablecloth, throw or pretty tea towel clipped to a pole will do the trick in next to no time. There are, of course, a number of more involved projects to really test your skills! Whichever project you choose, there will always be the reward of designing and creating your very own look and the chance to work with a wonderful array of fabric colours and textures.

This practical book contains a myriad of window treatments from the simplest of ready-made panels and elegant drapes to pretty tie tops and easy lined curtains. There are over twenty projects and many are accompanied by variations to inspire you to develop your own ideas. The eye-catching designs are simply explained, with illustrated step-by-step instructions, and each project is designed with an emphasis on speed and simplicity.

An introductory section features the equipment and materials needed for curtain-making followed by a section explaining all the basic techniques, from joining fabrics and sewing hems, to making casing and stylish mitred borders.

The book includes a wide variety of ideas to suit all tastes and budgets, some of which require no sewing at all to inspire even the least practical of people and concludes with a gallery packed with beautiful designs to inspire you to develop your own techniques and ideas to create great window treatments.

the basics

basic sewing equipment

DRESSMAKER'S SCISSORS

Bent-handled dressmaker's scissors or shears are the most comfortable to use for cutting fabric accurately as the angle of the handle allows the fabric to lie flat.

DRESSMAKING PINS

Pins are available with metal, glass or pearlized heads. Pins with coloured heads are easier to spot and pick up, though selecting pins which are fine and sharp is the main importance.

RULER

A metal or plastic ruler is a must-have and is handy to measure and mark short distances, and as a guide for drawing straight lines.

SMALL SCISSORS OR SNIPS

Small sharp scissors or special snips are useful for snipping thread ends and can be used close to the fabric where larger scissors would be unwieldy.

ERASABLE MARKER

Air- and water-erasable marker pens are easily available and are a useful addition to your sewing kit. Air-erasable marks will disappear after a fairly short time. Water-erasable marks remain until touched with water.

TAPE MEASURE

A plastic-coated or cloth tape measure is used to measure longer distances and around curves. A retractable tape measure is a neat option.

NEEDLES

Various types of needle are available and a mixed pack of multi-purpose needles is often the best option. Choose needles that are fine and sharp with eyes large enough to thread easily. Extra-fine needles are also available.

curtain-making equipment

HEADING TAPE

A stiff tape available in different widths and styles that is stitched to the top of curtains and pulled up to form pleats or gathers.

CURTAIN RINGS

Rings made from metal, plastic or wood which are attached to the top of the curtain and threaded onto a pole which the curtain is hung from.

CURTAIN HOOKS

Usually made from plastic, these are hooked into the back of the curtain heading tape and attached either directly to a curtain track or hooked onto the bottom of curtain rings. Curtain hooks are not usually visible.

EYELETS

Chrome or brass metal rings used to create holes in fabric to thread a pole or cord through, or simply as a decorative feature. Holes are made with a hole maker, which is usually supplied with the eyelet kit.

CURTAIN WEIGHTS

These are added inside a curtain's hem to add weight to the hem so that the curtain hangs better. Round coin-like weights can be added at each seam and side edge, or long chain weights can be threaded through the inside fold of the hem.

THREADS

Multi-purpose polyester thread is widely available in a wide range of colours for use on all types of fabric. Cotton thread is also available for cotton and wool fabrics, and silk thread for silk and wool fabrics.

STRIP VELCRO

A strip fastening that has two halves – one with a stiffer hooked surface and the other a softer looped surface. When pressed together the two halves interlock and stick to each other.

RIBBONS

Narrow strips or bands of fabric available in various widths and finishes such as satin and velvet. Satin ribbon can be single-faced with the satin finish on just one side or double-faced with a satin finish on both sides.

COTTON TAPE

A narrow strip or band of cotton fabric usually about 12–15 mm (½–⅝ in) wide used to finish edges and make ties.

the sewing machine

Most sewing machines are run by electricity through a foot pedal which is attached by one cable to the machine and another to the electricity supply. Pressure on the foot pedal will start the machine going and, as more pressure is added, the speed will increase. A hand wheel at the right of the machine is also usually employed when starting and stopping a piece of machine-stitching to help control the process.

Machine-stitching is formed from two threads: the top thread and the bobbin thread. Thread is first wound from the thread reel onto the bobbin by a system usually situated on the top of the machine. The top thread is then slotted through a number of guides and down and through the needle. The wound bobbin is placed into the bobbin case, which is under the needle. During the stitching process, the top thread forms the stitch on the top of the fabric and the bobbin thread forms the stitch on the underside with the two interlinking within the fabric.

Needles for sewing machines come in a variety of different sizes. The lower the number, the finer the needle point.

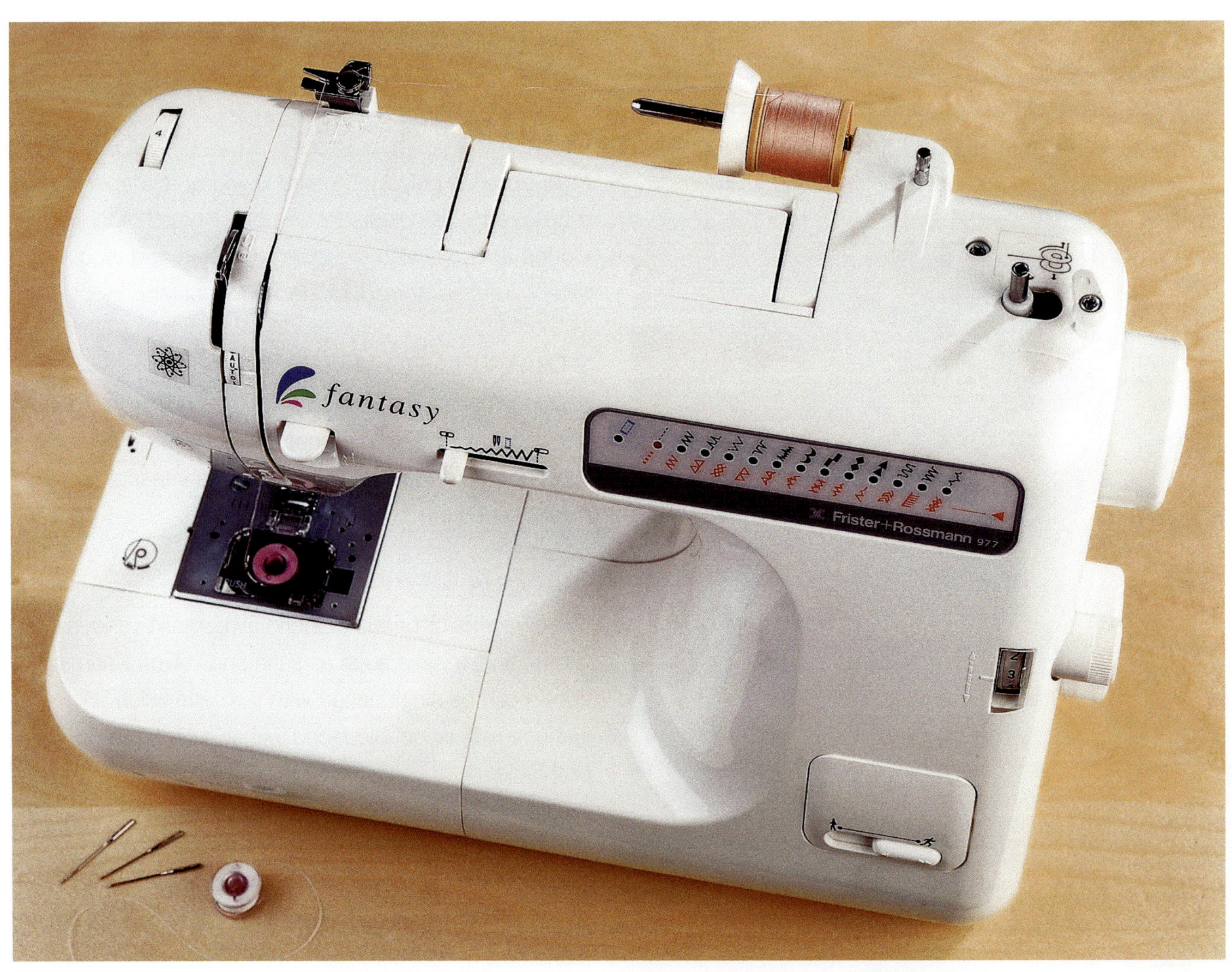

fabrics

COTTON

Cotton is one of the most popular fabrics as it is very versatile and is ideal for many of the projects in this book. A natural fabric made from the fluffy hairs that cover the seedpod of the cotton plant, it is available in light to medium weights.

Cotton fabrics handle well and do not fray. There are many different types of cotton fabric as they vary according to their weave and finish. Some of the most popular cotton fabrics include gingham, chambray, poplin, chintz, drill, ticking, cambric and toile de jouy. Lighter weight cottons include lawn and voile.

LINEN

Linen fabrics are made from the fibres of the flax plant and are woven into light to medium weight fabrics. Most linens resist fraying and handle well but are prone to creasing by virtue of the fabric's natural character. That said, the gorgeous sheen is often thought to offset this drawback and once the curtains are hung creasing will not be a problem.

SILK

Another beautiful natural fabric, silk is made from the pupae of the silk worm. Its inherent properties enable it to absorb dyes easily and this, together with its natural sheen, produce a wonderful range of deep, strong colours which cannot be achieved in other fabrics. It will crease a little more easily than cotton but presses well. Silk fabrics are more prone to fray and can be slippery to handle so a beginner who wants to use them is advised to start on a simple project. Silk dupion is a lightweight silk with a reasonably firm handle with a characteristic uneven slub weave which is part of its charm. Silk organza is very lightweight and see-through.

VOILE

This lightweight, translucent fabric drapes well. Voile can be made purely from cotton or from a mix of cotton and man-made fibre such as polyester to improve crease resistance.

LINING

Purpose-made cotton sateen is the most popular and widely used curtain lining. It has a slight sheen on the right side and comes in a range of colours. The lining colour can be chosen to match the curtain fabric or the traditional basic cream colour is usually cheaper and is widely used on all curtains. Special linings are also available, for example to totally block out light or to provide insulation.

basic techniques

The next few pages will guide you through all the essential techniques needed to complete the various projects in this book, from pinning and tacking to mastering seams and hems, and making decorative borders.

CUTTING OUT

When cutting out any curtain – except a curtain with a shaped top edge – it is important that the top edge is cut straight across the grain of the fabric. Most fabrics have finished side edges called selvedges and are made from two sets of threads: the warp thread which runs down the length of the fabric and the weft which runs across the width.

There are various ways to cut accurately across the grain. Fabrics with woven checks can be cut across following the line of the check. On loosely woven fabric, such as evenweave linen, a thread may be pulled out and then cut along that line. On other fabrics, such as a tightly-woven cotton, a line can be drawn with dressmaker's chalk or a sharp pencil across the fabric using a set square and a long ruler to ensure the line is at right angles to the side selvedges. If you do not have a set square, use a book or square object in its place. Place one edge exactly on the line of the side edge and place the ruler against the adjacent right angle edge. Draw the line along the ruler then cut along this line.

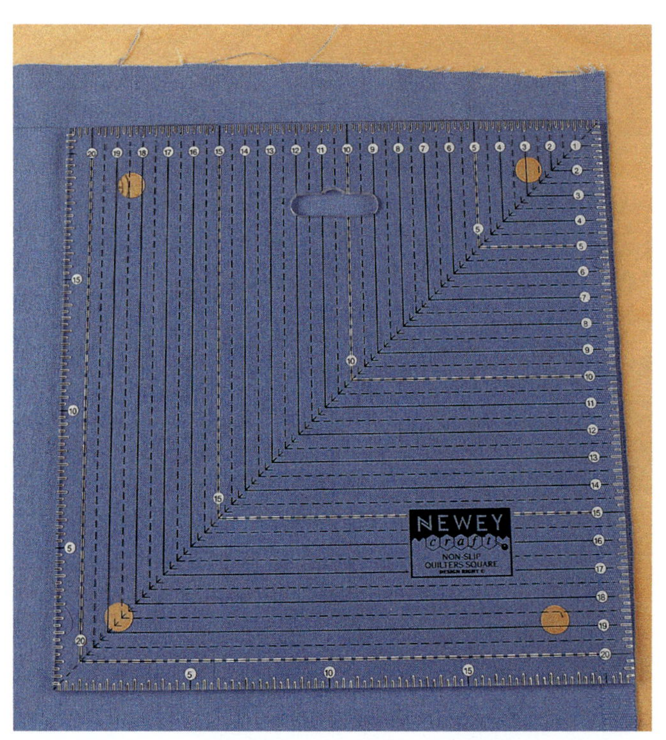

PINNING AND TACKING

CROSSWAYS PINNING

Place the edges to be joined together and pin the two layers together with pins at right angles to the edge. Place the pins about 5 cm (2 in) apart. On stiffer fabric, you can space them further apart. Pin diagonally when going around corners.

LENGTHWAYS PINNING

Lengthways pins are placed along the seam line where it will be stitched. When tacking or stitching, remove these pins as you reach them.

PINNING HEMS

Hems can be pinned with crossways pins or with pins lying in the same direction as the inner fold of the hem. Remove the pins when tacking or stitching, in the same way as before.

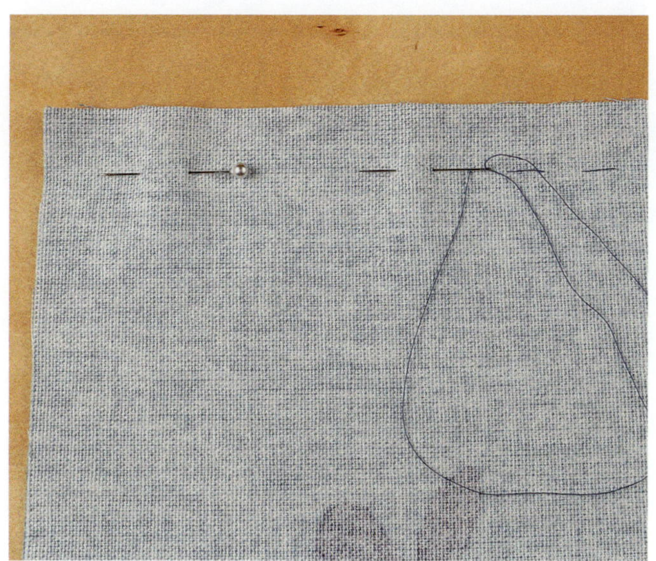

TACKING

Using sewing thread or special tacking thread, begin and finish tacking with one or two backstitches. Tack by stitching in and out through the layers of fabric, making stitches 1–1.5 cm (3/8–5/8 in) long. Work the tacking over crossways pins and remove the pins afterwards. On lengthways pinning, remove the pins as you reach them.

TACKING TO MATCH A PATTERN

Press the seam allowance, usually 1.5 cm (5/8 in), to the wrong side on one fabric edge. Overlap this over the other fabric edge by the same amount and arrange so the fabric pattern matches then pin in place. Knot the thread end then, working from the right side, tack the two edges together by taking a stitch in and out of the flat fabric next to the fold, then slipping the needle into and along inside the fold edge for a short way. Keep the stitches about 1 cm (3/8 in) long. Remove the pins and open the fold so the seam can be stitched from the wrong side.

stitches

A number of stitches are used in curtain making. Except for the zigzag stitch, all the stitches listed below are handstitches. A few simple hand stitches will add a fine finish to curtains and machine-stitched neatening will add durability.

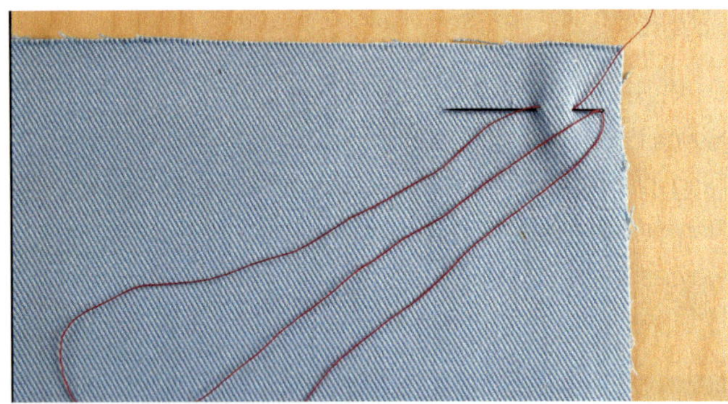

BACKSTITCH
Used to start and finish handstitching. When tacking, the stitches can be 6 mm (¼ in) long. In other areas, make them as small as possible. Insert the needle into the fabric and out again. Return the needle to the beginning and work one or two more stitches on top of the first one.

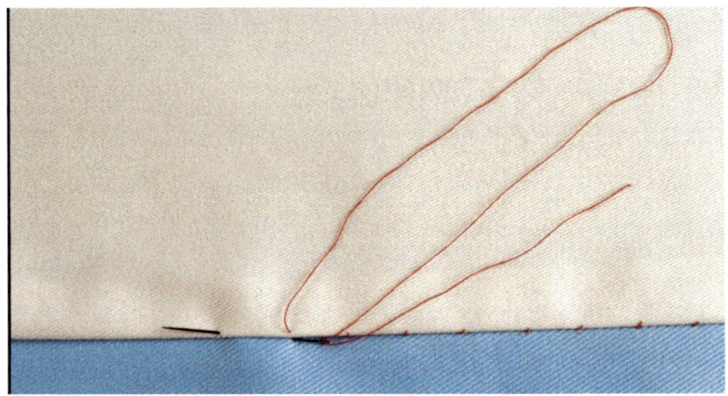

SLIPSTITCH
Used to sew lining to curtains. Make each stitch about 1.5 cm (⅝ in) long. Slide the needle along under the main fabric then out to pick up a couple of threads at the edge of the lining. Take the needle back to the main fabric and slide it along again to make the next stitch.

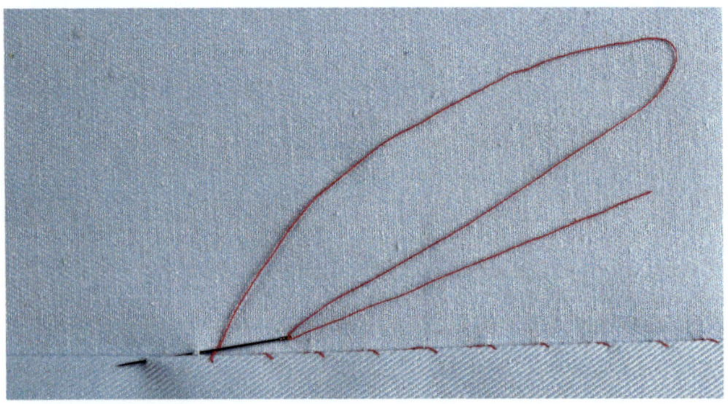

SLIP HEM
Used to stitch hems and the inner edge of bias binding. Begin with backstitches near the fold of the hem. Stitch across to pick up just a thread of fabric above the hem, then stitch along diagonally back through the hem. Repeat, taking care not to pull too tight. When stitching binding, instead of picking up a fabric thread, the stitch can pass through the back of the machine stitching.

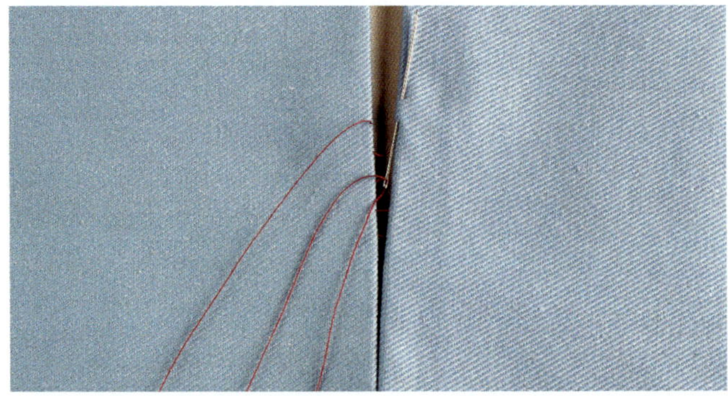

LADDER STITCH
This is used to stitch two butting folded edges together. Start with backstitches then take the needle along inside the fold of one edge for about 3–6 mm (⅛–¼ in). Bring the needle out at the fold, take it directly across to the other fold edge and stitch along inside that fold in the same way. Repeat.

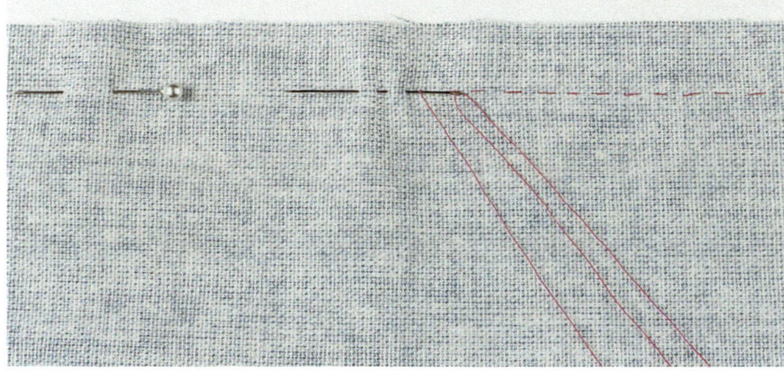

RUNNING STITCH

This simple handstitch is useful on small areas but is not very strong. Working from right to left, stitch along the seam line, taking the needle down through the two layers then back up again. Keep the stitches small.

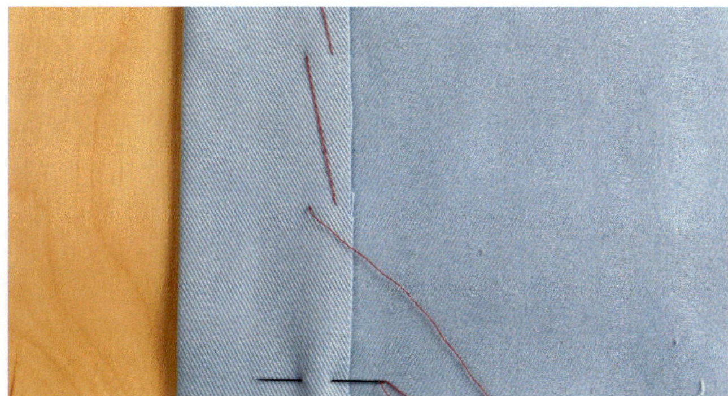

LONG STITCH

Used to stitch the side hems on interlined curtains where it holds the hem to the interlining. Make a horizontal stitch across from right to left, then take the needle down diagonally for about 4 cm (1½ in). Repeat.

HERRINGBONE STITCH

Used to stitch hems on interlined curtains. Work from left to right and begin with backstitches. Bring the needle through the hem, take it diagonally up to the right and take a stitch through above the hem from right to left. Bring the needle diagonally down to the right and take a stitch through the hem again from right to left. Repeat.

LOCKSTITCH

Used to stitch interlining to curtain fabric on interlined curtains. Fold back the interlining at the required position. Begin with backstitches on the interlining, then move the needle along and take a stitch through the fold of the interlining. Leave a loop of thread between the previous stitch and the needle eye and take a small stitch to pick up the curtain fabric within this loop. Pull the stitch through but do not pull it tight. Space the stitches at intervals of about 10 cm (4 in).

ZIGZAG STITCH

The zigzag stitch is a machine stitch and is worked over raw edges in order to make them neater and to prevent the fabric from fraying. The stitch length can be adjusted lengthways to space the stitches further apart or closer together. It can also be adjusted widthways to make the stitch wider or narrower. A medium stitch in both length and width is usually best for making the edges of a garment look neater. Zigzag stitch adjusted to make the stitches very close together is commonly known as satin stitch.

seams and hems

Whether you tack as well as pin your fabrics together before machining is a matter of personal preference. The less experienced may wish to pin and tack before stitching, while those with more confidence may prefer just to pin and remove the pins as the stitching reaches them.

PLAIN SEAM

A plain seam is used to join two pieces of fabric together. It can be pressed open when joining widths of fabric or left with the edges together. The seam allowance is usually 1.5 cm (5⁄8 in) wide. If it varies, this will be stated in the instructions.

1 Place the fabric pieces together with right sides facing and raw edges level. Stitch along 1.5 cm (5⁄8 in) in from the edge

2 Open out the fabric and press the seam open using the point of the iron. If the raw edges will be exposed, zigzag stitch along the edge to neaten.

NARROW SEAM

This type of seam is used on sheer fabrics as it is neater and less noticeable than a seam pressed open.

Stitch the seam as for a Plain seam (Step 1). Trim both seam allowances together to about half their original width. Zigzag stitch the two raw edges together. Open out the fabric and press the seam to one side.

trimming and snipping

The seam allowances are usually left intact but if they cause too much bulk at the edge of an item, they can be trimmed to about half their original width. To trim corners, first make a diagonal cut across the corner, then cut away wedges from either side of the diagonal cut.

FLAT FELL SEAM

A flat fell seam is used to join fabrics where a strong, easy-to-launder seam is required.

1 Place the two edges together with wrong sides facing and raw edges level. Stitch 1.5 cm (⅝ in) in from the edge. Trim one seam allowance to 6 mm (¼ in).

2 Open out the fabric and press the seam so the wider seam allowance lies on top of the trimmed one. Tuck the wider seam allowance under the trimmed edge and press. Stitch along close to the pressed fold by machine. The finished seam will have two rows of machine stitching on the right side.

BASIC HEM

Press 1–1.5 cm (3⁄8–5⁄8 in) to the wrong side, then press the hem depth to the wrong side and stitch in place by hand or machine.

DOUBLE HEM

This type of hem is used on sheer fabrics to conceal the inner layer of the hem. First press half the hem depth to the wrong side then press the same amount again and stitch in place by hand or machine.

ABOVE Use a double hem on sheer fabric so that the inner layer does not show through as a different depth.

BLIND HEM STITCHED HEM

Most machines have a blind hem stitch, which consists of a few straight stitches followed by a wide zigzag stitch. The straight stitches are worked along the hem edge and the zigzag stitch catches the hem to the main fabric. The stitch can be fiddly to set up accurately but is worth the effort when stitching long lengths.

Form the hem as described above. Then, with the wrong side uppermost, fold back the hem under the main fabric with the hem edge projecting and stitch in place.

MITRING A HEM

1 Press a hem of the required depth to the wrong side. Unfold the hem. At the side edge press the corner in at an angle on a line which begins at the side edge on the top fold and intersect the inner edge of the side hem at the lower fold.

2 Refold the hem so that it forms a neat mitre at the corner. Mitre the other corner in the same way. Handstitch the mitres in place and stitch the hem in place by hand or machine.

COVERING CURTAIN WEIGHTS

Coin weights are best covered to prevent them rubbing against the fabric. Fold a piece of lining fabric in half to make a pouch a little larger than the weight. Stitch together down the two side edges by hand or machine and slip the weight inside. Then stitch the two top corners of the pouch inside the inner fold of the hem.

professional tip

For long or heavy curtains, slip two weights into the pouch to add extra weight. If you need to make multiple pockets, cut a long strip and fold it in half lengthways. Stitch across near one end then leave the pocket space and stitch again to make the second row of pocket stitching. Leave a gap of about 1 cm (3/8 in) and stitch again to make the first row of the second pocket. Leave the pocket space and stitch again. Continue to make as many pockets as needed then separate by cutting between the 1 cm (3/8 in) apart rows of stitching.

borders and mitred borders

SINGLE STRAIGHT BORDER

The single border is formed on the front of the curtain only and can be used on curtains lined edge to edge as in the Sail curtains (pages 62–64). The border is stitched first to two opposite edges. The borders that are then stitched to the remaining two edges continue across the ends of the first borders. If the centre panel is rectangular, stitch the two longer edges first.

Measure the first two edges and cut borders to this length by the desired finished width plus 3 cm (1¼ in). With right sides facing, stitch the borders to the centre panel, taking 1.5 cm (⅝ in) seam allowances. Press the seams towards the borders. Measure the two remaining edges, including the ends of the first borders, and cut borders to this length and the same width. Stitch in place and press in the same way as the first borders.

LEFT A double border will add a neat contrast edging to a patterned curtain.

DOUBLE STRAIGHT BORDER

This double border fits over the edge of the curtain so you need to cut the curtain to the required finished size and cut the border four times the width you desire.

1 Press the borders in half then unfold and fold each side edge over so that they nearly meet at the centre, making one half of the border just slightly wider than the other. This slightly wider half will be the underneath half. Press in these creases.

2 Unfold the slightly narrower half of the top border and place it to the right side of the main panels with the raw edges level. Stitch in place along the pressed crease.

3 Fold the other half of the border over to the wrong side so the wider half overlaps the stitching slightly. Working from the right side, 'stitch in the ditch' by stitching along within the indentation of the previous seam to stitch the under layer.

finishing the ends

To finish the short ends neatly on a double border allow 0.5 cm (¼ in) extra to project beyond the edge before stitching the first row. After stitching the first row, fold the border first towards the edge, then fold the second fold edge back on itself level with the stitched line. Stitch across the projecting end level with the top of the curtain. Then turn the border right side out and stitch the second row of border stitching.

SINGLE MITRED BORDER

The single mitred border adds a decorative border around the main panel is ideal for curtains that are lined right out to the edges, as with the Sail curtains (pages 62–64). Decide the required finished width of the border and add on 3 cm (1¼ in). For the length, measure the length of the centre panel including seam allowances and add on twice the width of the finished border.

1 Mark and match the centre of the borders to the centre of the edges to which they are being stitched. Stitch the border to the edges, starting and finishing the stitching 1.5 cm (⅝ in) in from the edge of the centre panel. Keeping the ends of the previous border out of the way, stitch all four borders in this way.

2 At the corner, fold the centre panel diagonally so that the two borders adjoining the corner are level, and fold the seam allowance towards the centre panel. Place a ruler level with the diagonal fold and draw a stitching line across the border from the end of the previous stitching to the outer corner. Stitch along the line.

3 Stitch all four corners of the border the same way as Step 2. Draw a line 1.5 cm (⅝ in) outside the diagonal stitched line. Trim the corner away along the drawn line. Trim all four corners in this way.

4 Open out the borders and press the diagonal corner seam allowances open. The long straight border seam allowances can be pressed open to reduce bulk on thicker fabric or both the seam allowances can be pressed towards the border, as shown, which generally looks better.

DOUBLE MITRED BORDER

This type of border projects outside the edge of the curtain. To calculate the width to cut the borders, decide on the desired finished width of the border, double this and add on 3 cm (1¼ in) seam allowances. For the length, measure the length of the centre panel including seam allowances plus twice the width of the finished border.

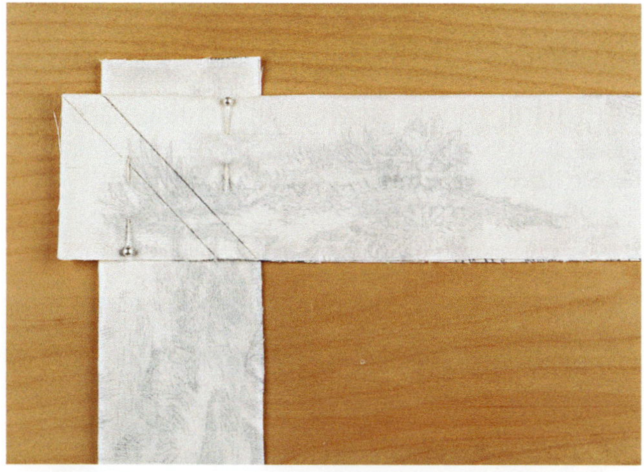

1 Fold the borders in half with the wrong sides outside. Overlap the ends of two borders at right angles, with the fold edges on the outer edges and the ends projecting by 1.5 cm (⅝ in), and pin. Draw a seam line diagonally across the corner between the points where the borders intersect. Mark the seam allowance 1 cm (⅜ in) outside the seam line. Turn the border over and repeat on the other side. Trim along the outer lines.

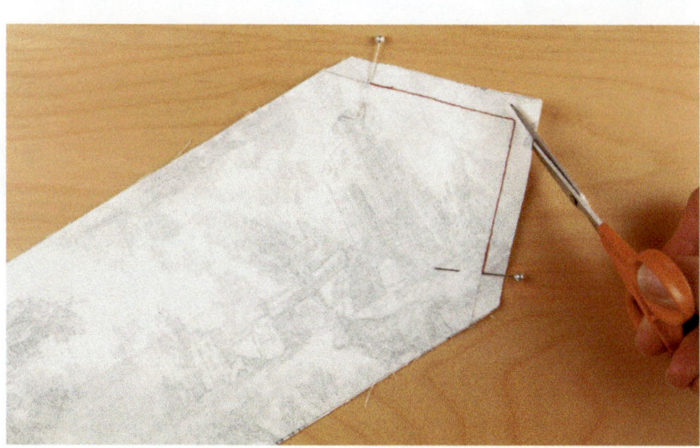

2 Unpin the borders. Open them out and mark the seam line on the unmarked half of each border. Place the appropriate two borders together with right sides facing and stitch along the marked lines, starting and finishing 1.5 cm (⅝ in) in from the side edges of the border. Trim the point and press the seam open. Stitch all four corners in this way.

3 Place the right side of one border edge to the wrong side of the centre panel. Pin together, making sure all four corners match, so that the end of the border stitching is 1.5 cm (⅝ in) from each edge at the corners. Stitch each edge separately, stopping and restarting at each corner.

4 Press the seam allowance to the wrong side along the remaining edge of the border, then place it over to the right side of the centre panel so that it just covers the previous stitching and the seam is enclosed. Stitch in place.

casings

Casings form channels at the top of a curtain through which a pole or tension rod is treaded to create ruffles. The casing can be sewn at the edge of the fabric or it can be positioned just in from the edge so that a frill forms above when it is drawn up. A casing can also be cut from a separate strip of fabric.

FOLD-OVER CASING

This simple casing provides a channel to thread through a pole or tension rod.

1 First press 1 cm (⅜ in) to the wrong side, then press the depth of the casing to the wrong side. Pin and tack in place.

2 Machine stitch in place along the lower edge. You can also machine stitch a second row of stitches around the top of the casing to give it a neat finish.

SELF-FRILL CASING

This type of casing is similar to the fold-over casing but here the channels are stitched in from the edge so that a frill of fabric stands up above the casing.

1 First press 1 cm (3/8 in) to the wrong side, then press the depth of the casing plus the depth of the frill over to the wrong side. Pin, tack, then machine stitch in place along the lower edge of the casing.

2 Stitch a second row about 2–3 cm (3/4–1 1/4 in) above the first to form the casing channel.

OPPOSITE A self-frill casing standing up above the pole adds an attractive detail to a café curtain.

SEPARATE CASING

These casings are made from a separate strip of fabric. Cut the strip the required length and depth of the casing plus 2 cm (3/4 in) on the length and 2.5 cm (1 in) on the depth.

1 Press 1 cm (3/8 in) to the wrong side along the long lower edge of the casing. Place the casing to the edge of the curtain with right sides facing, long raw edges level and the short ends projecting 1 cm (3/8 in) at each side edge. Pin, tack then stitch in place 1.5 cm (5/8 in) in from the edge of the curtain.

2 Press the stitched seam allowances onto the casing and press the projecting ends onto the wrong side of the casing level with the side edges. Press the casing over to the wrong side. Pin, tack and machine stitch in place along the lower edge.

fringing

Fringing can be bought as a trim or made by pulling away the threads from a woven fabric. Some woven fabrics, such as tightly-woven fabrics and drill do not fringe well so check before purchasing.

APPLYING FRINGING TRIM

1 Press a narrow turning, just wide enough to be covered by the braid part of the fringe, onto the right side.

2 Lay the fringing braid along the turning to cover it. Stitch in place with a row of stitching near the fabric edge and another just above the raw edge so that it is enclosed.

FRINGING FABRIC

1 For a more durable fringe, first stitch a row of narrow zigzag stitching across the fabric at the top of the fringe.

2 A fringe can be made by pulling the horizontal fabric threads away from the fabric edge all the way to the zigzag stitching line.

tucks

Tucks are stitched folds of fabric formed for a decorative effect. When using tucks, the fabric is reduced by twice the depth of the tuck. Tucks are a good way to reduce the length when bought items, such as a sheet, are used as curtains.

MAKING PIN TUCKS

Fold the fabric along the line of the tuck with wrong sides facing and press along the fold. With the fabric still folded, stitch along 3 mm (⅛ in) in from the fold using the machine foot as a guide. Open out the fabric and press the tuck to one side.

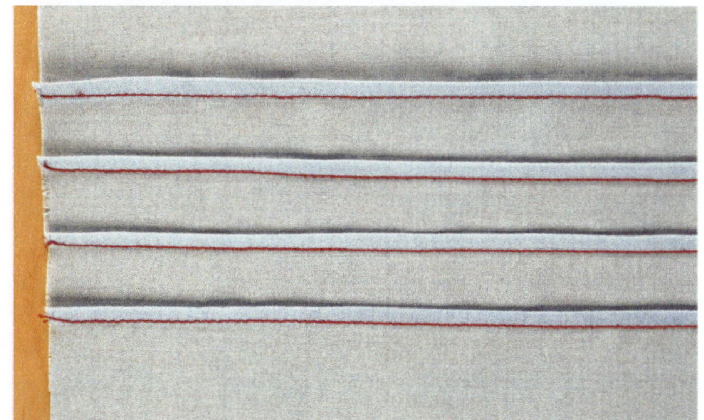

A series of parallel pin tucks are more effective than single ones. To space the tucks evenly, first mark the distance between the tucks with pins or an erasable marker, then fold along the marked line and press the fold of the new tuck removing the pins as you reach them.

WIDE TUCKS

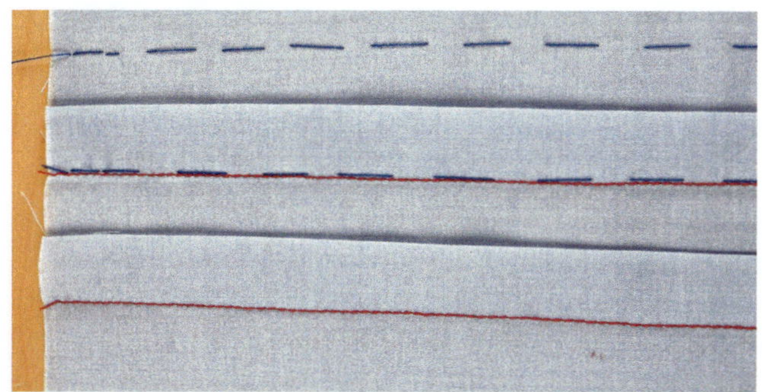

Fold the fabric along the line of the tuck and press along the fold. Measure the depth of the tuck away from the fold with pins. Tack, then stitch along the tacked line. Alternatively, stitch keeping the fabric fold against one of the guidelines on the plate beside the machine foot to keep the stitching an even distance in from the fold. Open out the fabric and press the tuck to one side.

TWIN NEEDLE TUCKS

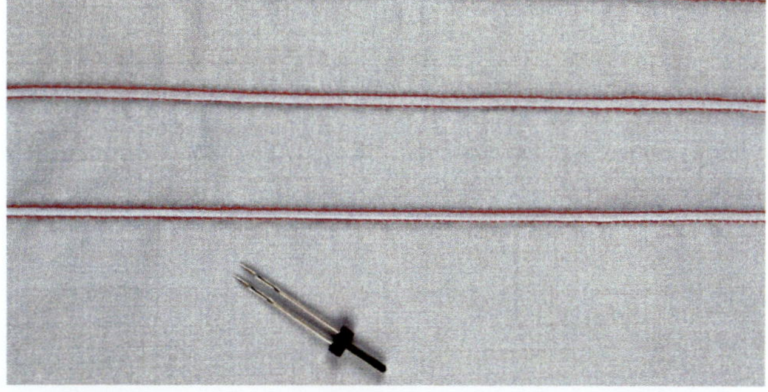

A machine twin needle, which stitches two parallel rows, gives a fine tucked effect on lightweight fabric such as lawn. First press a crease to form a line for the tuck. Open out the fabric and stitch along the pressed crease so that it is central between the two needles.

finishing touches

Eyelets, ties and curtain rings are good alternatives to traditional heading tape for hanging curtains from a pole. Curtain rings and ties can be stitched directly to the curtain and eyelets can be threaded on a pole or hung from hooks.

STITCHING ON CURTAIN RINGS

Stitch the small lower curtain eyelet ring by hand to the back of the top edge of the curtain at the positions marked with pins. The lower edge of the ring can be stitched at the top edge of the curtain so that it remains visible, or it can be stitched lower down so that it is partly hidden by the curtain and mainly just the larger ring shows. Work small stitches side by side over the ring and through the back layer of the curtain fabric.

MAKING TIES

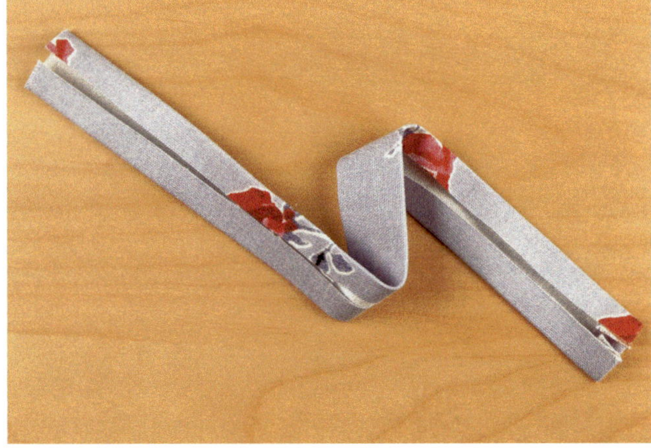

1 Press 1 cm (⅜ in) to the wrong side across one short end, or both ends if they are exposed, and along both long edges.

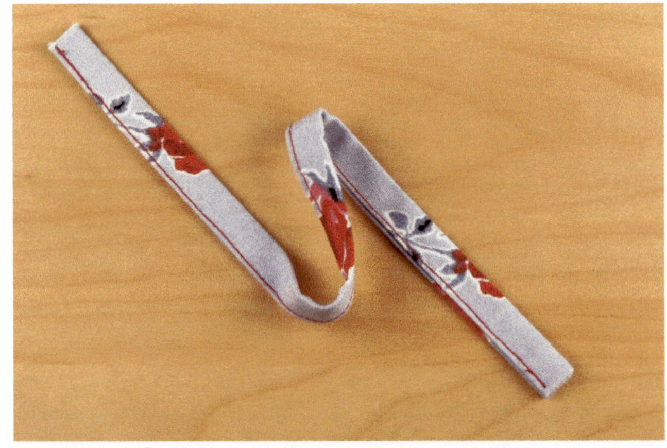

2 Fold the tie in half lengthways and press again. Stitch down the length of the tie. On wide ties, stitch across the pressed end as well. On narrow 12-mm (½-in) wide ties, the end can be left unstitched.

EYELET HOLES AND SPACING

1 Mark the position for the eyelets at each end, about 2 cm (¾ in) in from the side edges, with vertical pins. Place out the eyelets evenly between so they are about 13–15 cm (5–6 in) apart. Then reduce or increase the distance between as required to fit the curtain width.

2 When the eyelets' positions are all evenly spaced, mark with a cross at the centre and remove the pins. Place the fabric on the disc provided and position the cutting tool over the marked cross. Cut the hole following the manufacturer's instructions.

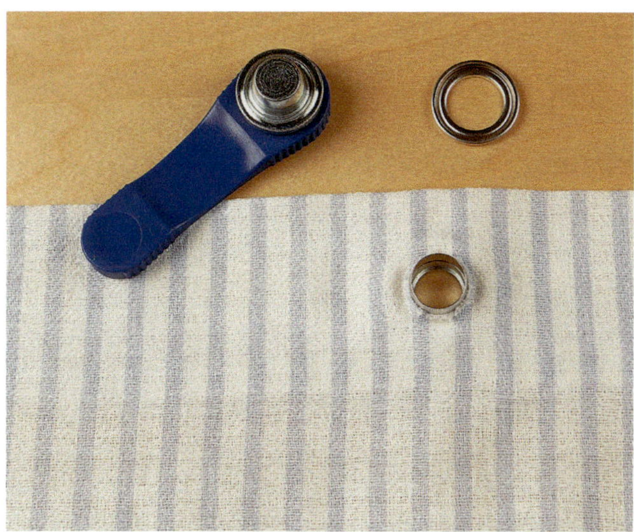

3 Working on a firm surface, turn the disc over. Place the eyelet on the disc then place the fabric, right side down, onto the eyelet so it protrudes through the cut hole.

4 Press the washer with its closed side upwards onto the eyelet. Position the die on the assembling tool provided over the assembled eyelet. Check all is aligned and hammer in place following the manufacturer's instructions.

making tie-backs

Tie-backs are used to hold curtains away from the window, either to let in more light or simply to create a pleasing draped effect. For the simplest of tie-backs, ribbon or cord can be looped around the curtain and fastened onto a wall hook beside or behind the curtain. Straight tie-backs are almost as easy to make and add a stylish finish.

STRAIGHT TIE-BACK

This simple straight tie-back is fastened with eyelets which can be tied together to fasten with ribbon, cotton tape or a white shoelace, or just fastened onto a wall hook. Alternatively the tie-back can be made with curtain rings instead stitched to the centre at either end to attach to a wall hook.

MATERIALS
Fabric
Sewing thread
Heavy-weight iron-on interfacing
2 eyelets per tie-back or 2 curtain rings

CUTTING OUT
1.5 cm (⅝ in) seam allowances are included unless instructions state otherwise. Cut the tie-back 10 cm (4 in) wide by the required length plus 3 cm (⅝ in). Cut the interfacing to same length but half the width.

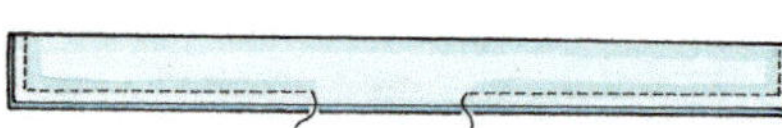

1 Iron on the interfacing following the manufacturer's instructions lengthways to half the fabric. Fold the fabric in half lengthways over it. Stitch across each end and along the long edge leaving a 10-cm (4-in) opening partway along the long edge.

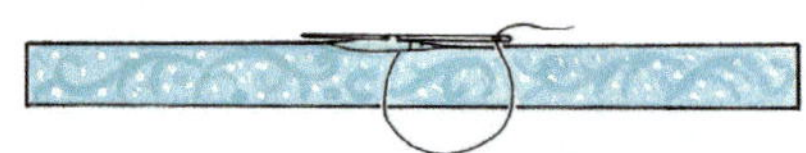

2 Trim the interfacing from the seam allowances then the seams and corners. Turn the tie-back right side out, press the seam at the edge and the seam allowance inside along the opening. Slipstitch the opening closed.

3 Stitch a curtain ring to the centre of each end in the same way as you would with a curtain. Alternatively, attach an eyelet centrally at either end of the tie-back following the manufacturer's instructions and fasten onto a wall hook.

hanging devices

Curtains are hung traditionally from tracks or poles attached near the top of the window. Curtain tracks tend to be purely functional and are attached near the top of the window frame, while poles are decorative as well as functional and are usually attached to the wall above the window. Other lighter weight poles are available for voiles, nets and half-length café curtains.

CURTAIN POLE

Curtain poles come in many styles of metal and wood, often with decorative finials fitted to either end. Poles are fixed by brackets usually on the wall above the window. Rings, which are stitched to the top of the curtain, are threaded onto the pole to hang the curtain below the pole. Alternatively, spring clips can be attached to the curtains and hooked onto the rings.

CAFÉ CURTAIN POLE

An adjustable lightweight pole for hanging café curtains and other lightweight curtains. This is fixed flat to the window and, unlike a tension rod, does not need a reveal or recess to fit into.

CURTAIN RAIL OR TRACK

A conventional track is usually made of plastic and is used in conjunction with heading tape and curtain hooks. The heading tape is stitched to the top of the curtain and hooks are then threaded onto the tape and attached to run along the track. When closed, the curtain covers the track and the top of the curtain protrudes above it

TENSION WIRE

This is a fine-coiled metal wire covered with white plastic. This is threaded through a casing either just at the top, or at the top and bottom of the curtain and small metal eyes are screwed into each end. These are in turn fastened to matching metal hooks, which screw to the window surround.

ABOVE Decorative finials give a stylish finish to the end of curtain poles.

TENSION ROD OR POLE

An adjustable rod with a spring fixing which holds it under tension between the side edges of a window frame or recess. Ideal for lightweight curtains and café curtains.

types of windows

There are many different types of windows varying with the style and the period of the property, from huge plain glass picture windows to tiny mullioned recess windows. These are a few of the most common.

SASH WINDOW

Sash windows open by sliding up and down on rope pulleys which are concealed inside boxes in the sides.

CASEMENT WINDOW

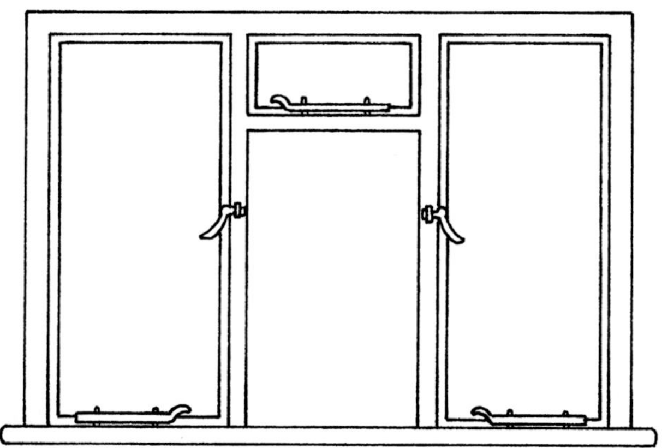

Casement windows open on hinges at one side. Vertical windows are usually hinged at the side and small top ventilation windows are hinged at the top.

RECESSED WINDOW

Recessed windows are set back into the wall so that they are level or nearly level with the outside of the wall and have a deep sill at the front. They usually have casement type openings.

BAY WINDOW

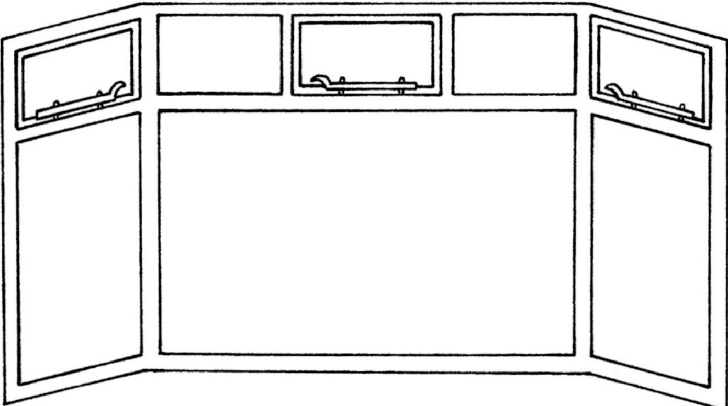

Bay windows project from the wall of the room forming an alcove within the room. The shape of the bay can be curved, angled or square and the windows may be sash or casement.

design and effect

First consider the overall effect you are looking to create in the design of the curtain and the density of the fabric before deciding on what type of fabric and how much of it you need to buy.

WINDOW TREATMENTS

RECESSED WINDOWS

These types of window have the option of the curtain being fitted either inside or outside the recess. The former will require a smaller curtain but the curtain will obscure some of the window even when it is fully drawn or tied back. To obtain maximum light, fit curtains outside the recess or consider a blind as an alternative within.

Curtains hung outside the recess will give a grander dressing and can be made to draw right back and hang to just below the sill or to floor level.

Curtains hung inside a recess will cover some of the glass even when tied back and will give a cosy cottage look.

CASEMENT WINDOWS

The style chosen for the curtains can affect the look of a window. A casement window can be given the appearance of a smaller, more cottagey window by dressing it with a single curtain pulled back to one side, or the window can be made to look larger with curtains stacked back at either side.

A double layer swag is an effective window treatment for a casement window in a small room such as a ground floor bathroom where more privacy may be required.

In a larger room, curtains hung from a long pole so that they stack back either side of the window to just cover the frame will make the same size window look wider and give a more contemporary look.

dressing windows

The window to be dressed can be partly or wholly obscured by the curtain. This will cut out some light but will hide an unsightly view or provide privacy. A lightweight see-through fabric such as voile or fine linen will let a good percentage of light through. For curtains that are to be drawn back, thinner fabric will take up less space when pulled back than denser fabric, which may cover the sides of the window. If you can, fit a rail or pole that is wider than the window so when the curtain is drawn back it hangs over the wall and window frame and no glass is obscured. The area the curtain covers when it is pulled back is called the stack back.

Curtains fitted outside the recess to cover the whole window frame can be hung from a rail attached to the window trim or a pole fitted above the window on the wall. Before measuring up fabric quantities, the curtain fixing method should be considered as it will affect both the width and length of the curtain.

BAY WINDOWS

On large windows and bay windows a pair of curtain can be made to pull around the whole bay from the two side edges to meet at the centre. However this will probably mean the curtain will cover quite a large area of the window even when pulled right back, and the curtain may be difficult to draw. An option is to divide the curtain into four smaller widths so each has less distance to travel when drawn.

On bay windows, a single pair of curtains made to cover the whole window will cover some of the window even when pulled right back. Sill-length curtains will emphasize the width or the window.

On bay windows, four curtain sections can often be arranged to let in more light and may draw more easily. Floor-length curtains will emphasize the height of the window and make it look taller than sill-length curtain.

CAFÉ CURTAINS

Half curtains that cover just the lower half on the window are generally known as café curtains. These can be made to fit across the whole width of the window and hung on a lightweight pole, tension wire or special café curtain pole fixed to the window frame. Alternatively, the curtain can be made to cover just the glazed area of the window and hung from a tension rod wedged in place between the window jambs at either side.

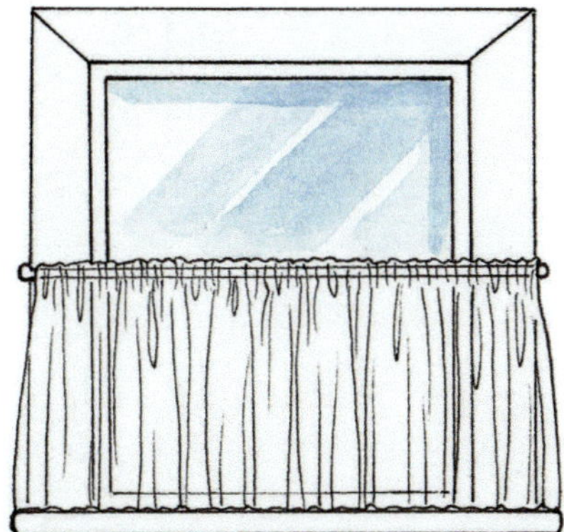

A café curtain can be hung from a lightweight pole fixed to the window frame at either side.

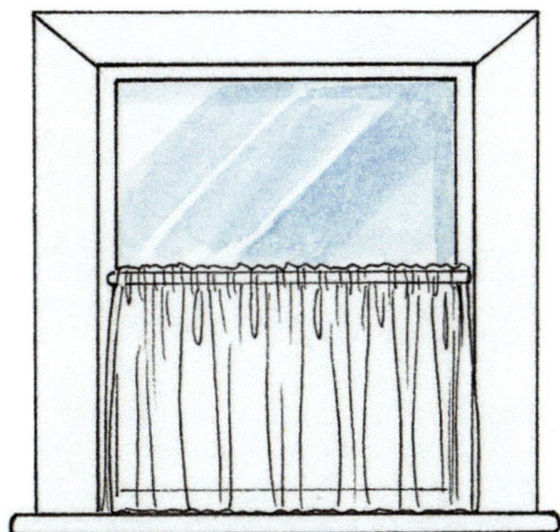

Alternatively, café curtains can be made to cover just the glazed area and fitted in place on a tension rod between the widow jambs.

measuring up

Take the measurements carefully – it often helps to have a friend to hold the end of the measuring tape, particularly on large windows. Not all the measurements below will be needed according to the style of the curtain.

CALCULATING FABRIC QUANTITIES

Measure up carefully and double check your measurements to make sure your figures are correct. Furnishing fabrics are quite wide so often one width of fabric is enough for many windows. You will find that the staff at most furnishing fabric counters are very helpful and will help check your figures if you are in doubt.

INSIDE A RECESS

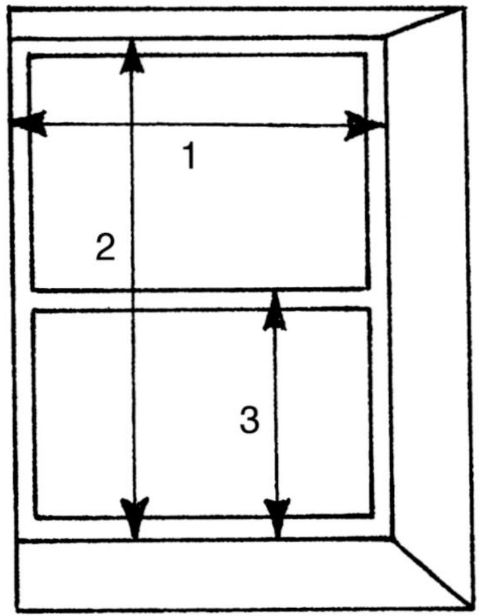

1 Width inside recess
2 Length inside recess
3 Length from glazing bar to sill for a café curtain

OUTSIDE A RECESS OR REVEAL

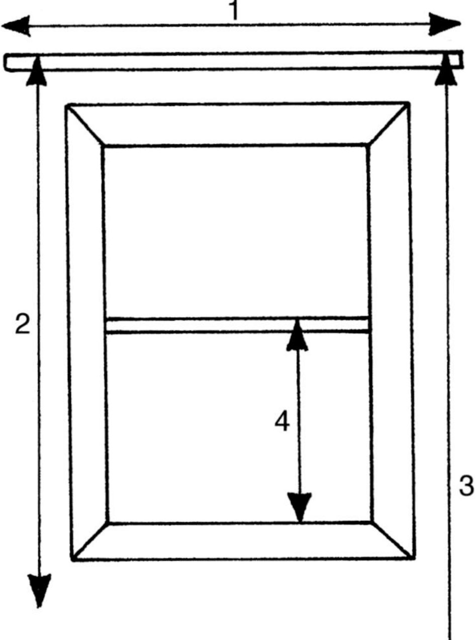

1 Length of curtain pole or rail
2 Length from pole or rail to lower edge of curtain
3 Length from pole or rail to floor
4 Length from glazing bar to sill for a café curtain

ESTIMATING FABRIC

The amount of fabric needed for a window will depend on the style of curtain being made. The three main factors to consider are:

- the size of the window
- the style of the curtain
- the fullness of the curtain

Before finalizing your measurements, you will need to consider the position and length of the pole or track, and the style and finished length of the curtain. The precise length can be finalized after the curtain has been made and hung but you will need to establish a required length before you can cut out.

FULLNESS

The fullness of the curtain required will determine the number of widths or part widths needed for each curtain. Most full curtains look best with at least double fullness, so multiply the length of the pole or track by two to get the total width needed. Short curtains that don't need too much weight to hang well and can be made with less fullness, as can curtains for a recess where too much fullness may block out the light. Also, if a fabric with a large overall and dominant pattern is chosen, less fullness is needed so that the fabric design is not obscured by the folds of fullness. Consult the table below for ideal fullness amounts:

HEADING	FULLNESS
Tie top	1½–2 times
Tab top	1½–2 times
Curtain ring top	2–2½ times
Gathered	2–2½ times on most fabrics, 2½–3 on voiles
Pencil pleated	2–2½ times
Triple pleat	2–2½ times

FABRIC WIDTHS

The following example shows how to estimate the number of fabric widths needed to make a pair of curtains. Whole fabric widths do not have to be joined, for example, each curtain could have one and a half widths so a total of three widths would be required. It is often not worth going smaller than a half width, though if the remaining fabric can be used, a quarter width can be added.

Total pole or track length for two curtains	= 200 cm
Divide by two to get width of one curtain	= 100 cm
Add on amount required for two side hem	= 110 cm
Multiply by the required fullness (eg. x 2½)	= 275 cm
Divide by the width of the fabric (eg.140 cm)	= 1.96
Round up or down to the nearest whole or half fabric width	= 2 widths per curtain

PATTERN REPEATS

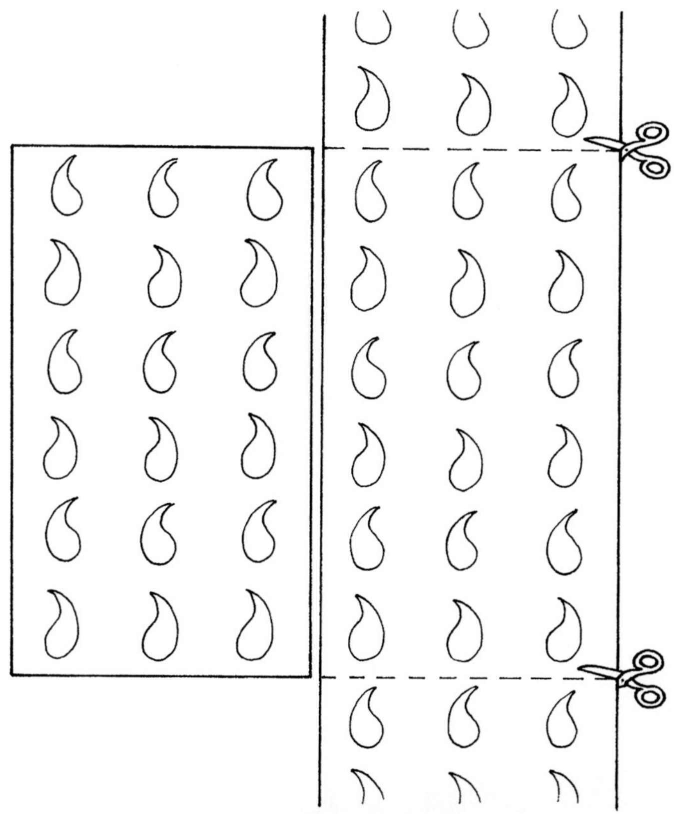

Fabric printed with small, all-over patterns will probably not need matching. However, larger patterns (when you can see the same part of the design repeated a distance away) will need to be matched when joining widths and also on each curtain so that the pattern is at the same level on each curtain when the curtains are drawn.

The distance between where the same part of the design is printed again is called the repeat. The distance or the amount of the repeat is sometimes marked on the side edge of the fabric. You need to add the length of the repeat to each fabric length of each width so the pattern can be matched across all lengths. The simplest way to do this is to cut the length required for the first width, then lay out the fabric of the next length next to it, arranging the repeat so that it matches. This will show exactly what fabric needs to be trimmed away to begin the next length.

projects

clip top

The simplest of all, non-sew clip top curtains, use ready-made items instead of fabric – sheets, bedspreads, throws, tablecloths and even tea towels can be chosen according to the size of the window and the thickness you want the curtain to be. Small clips in the form of tiny pegs, spirals or flat spring clips are clipped to the curtain, some then hook onto curtain rings while others incorporate their own ring.

MATERIALS

Ready-made item, such as a sheet, tablecloth or throw

Clips

HANGING DEVICE

Pole and finials, rod or tension wire and metal screw eyes and hooks

SUITS...

Cotton, polycotton, chambray and velour fabrics

Flat and recess windows

MAKING UP

Choose the item for your curtain as near as you can to fit the space to be filled. The width can be adjusted by adding more or less fullness. If you wish the curtain to hang with fullness, you will need to allow about twice the required width for the fullness. The length can be adjusted by raising the pole or by allowing the curtain to hang below the sill or, for extra length, to puddle on the floor. Alternatively, the length can be adjusted by folding over the top edge or, on lightweight, plain fabrics such as sheets and tablecloths, a series of tucks can be stitched cross the width and will be very effective against the light.

To make the tucks, just fold the fabric with its wrong sides together and stitch along an even distance from the fold. Each tuck will take up twice the amount you stitch from the fold. Try a series of three a little up from the base of the piece making each lower tuck wider than the one above.

FLORAL PANEL

A tablecloth with a bold border and central posies of stylized flowers makes a fresh window treatment for a plain room. Choose the cloth in a size to suit and hang it with clip-on pegs hooked onto the curtain rings.

SPIRALS AND STRIPES

This ready-made curtain is a tea towel with small spiral metal coils threaded through it at intervals across the top edge. These then just thread through the curtain rings on the pole.

ready-made fold-over top

Simple but effective, a fold-over top is a quick and easy way to shorten the length of ready-made items to fit the window. As for the clip top curtain, all manner of sheets, cloths and throws can be used successfully. However, as the fold-over area will show the other side of the fabric, it will need to look the same on both right and reverse sides or have a reverse side which will work attractively with the right side.

MATERIALS

Ready-made item, such as a sheet, tablecloth or throw
Clip-on rings or curtain rings

HANGING DEVICE

Pole and finials

SUITS...

Cotton, polycotton, chambray, silk and linen fabrics
Flat and recess windows

MAKING UP

Simply fold the excess fabric over to the right side to hang down in a second layer. Fasten a couple of clips or pin curtain rings to the fold then slip the rings onto the pole, holding the folded piece against the window to check the length is alright. Remove from the window and press along the fold.

Arrange the position of the clips or rings across the top edge, placing one near each side edge and the others spaced evenly between, about 12.5–15 cm (5–6 in) apart. If using curtain rings, mark the position with pins. Stitch the lower edge of the rings neatly to the fold edge or lower down so that they are partly hidden by the curtain. Work small stitches side by side over the rings and through the back layer of the fold, removing the pins as you go. If the rings have a small eyelet ring, stitch this by hand to the back of the top edge of the fold.

Fold–over curtains can also be made speedily from fabric. Choose a fabric width so that the ready finished selvedges can be used for the side edges and make a double hem along the lower edge and the fold-over.

TIE-TRIMMED CLOTH

A tablecloth with decorative lacework or a pretty scalloped border can be tied to a pole with ribbons or tapes for a fresh window treatment.

First hold up the cloth and decide how much needs to fold back to make the cloth to the required length for the window. Fold the required amount down onto the right side of the cloth and press to make the crease. Decide on the length of the ties and cut each one twice the finished length. Fold the ties in half and crease to mark the fold. Unfold the cloth and the ties. Lay the ties across the fold line so that the fold on both ties and cloth match. Arrange the ties evenly with one near each end. Finally machine stitch the ties in place along the fold line and refold the curtain.

BEADED STRIPES

A colourful tablecloth boldly striped in a medley of mauves and lilac is a great choice for a simple fold-over curtain. The deep fold-over border at the top is almost half the curtain depth giving an attractive two-tier effect. The cloth has a pretty beaded border all round and this gives a ready-made edging along the base of the fold-over section. Spaced clips attached to curtain rings are ideal for hanging this quick window treatment.

sewn fold-over top

This method is suitable where a fold-over top is required on curtains with different right and wrong sides, where the fold-over section needs to be cut as a separate piece. It can also be used when you wish to add a contrast fabric for the fold-over section or use stripes cut in the opposite direction.

MATERIALS
Fabric
Contrast fabric
Sewing thread

HANGING DEVICE
Pole and finials
Curtain rings

SUITS...
Cotton and polycotton fabrics
Flat and recess windows

CUTTING OUT

Decide on the required finished length of the curtain and add on 11.5 cm (4½ in) for hem and seam allowances. Decide on the length of the fold-over and add on 5.5 cm (2⅛ in) for hem and seam allowances. For the width allow 1⅓ to 2 times the width for fullness – the lighter the fabric, the more fullness it can have – plus 8 cm (3¼ in) for side hems.

METHOD

1 Press 1 cm (⅜ in) then 3 cm (1¼ in) deep hems to the wrong side down each side edge of the main piece and machine stitch in place. Then press a double 5-cm (2-in) hem to the wrong side across the lower edge and machine stitch in place.

2 Press 1 cm (⅜ in) then 3-cm (1¼-in) deep hems to the wrong side down each side edge of the fold-over piece and machine stitch in place. In the same way stitch a 3-cm (1¼-in) deep hem to the wrong side along the lower edge of the fold-over section.

3 Place the fold-over section to the top edge of the main panel so the right side of the fold-over faces the wrong side of the main piece and the top-edges are level. Stitch in place 1.5 cm (⅝ in) down from the top edge.

4 Press the seam open, then fold the fold-over over the right side so that the seam is at the top edge and press again. Stitch curtain rings to the top edge, one near each end, and the others spaced evenly between, about 12.5–15 cm (5–6 in) apart.

rope top

Loops of rope swirl along the top of a cool check fabric to add texture and style to a smart bathroom curtain. The ends of the rope tuck neatly into the side hems and the rope is hand stitched to the top edge with loops formed at intervals to make rope rings to thread onto the curtain pole. Choose a fairly soft pliable rope – a cotton washing line or thick piping cord from the haberdashery department could be used.

MATERIALS
Fabric
Rope about 3 times curtain width plus 30 cm (12 in)
Sewing thread

HANGING DEVICE
Café curtain pole

SUITS...
Lightweight cotton, polycotton, pique and linen fabrics
Flat and recess windows

CUTTING OUT

1.5 cm (⅝ in) seam allowances are included unless the instructions state otherwise. Measure the required curtain width and add the required amount for fullness plus 10 cm (4 in) for side hems. Measure the required length and add on 21 cm (8¼ in).

METHOD

1 Press 1 cm (⅜ in) then another 4 cm (1½ in) to the wrong side across the top edge and machine stitch in place. Topstitch along the top edge.

2 Press 2.5 cm (1 in) then another 2.5-cm (1-in) hem to the wrong side down the side edges of the curtain and machine stitch in place.

3 Tuck the ends of the rope inside the top of the left side hem for about 2.5 cm (1 in) near the fold. Hand stitch in place through rope from the front top edge to the back top edge. Stitch through and back a few times to secure.

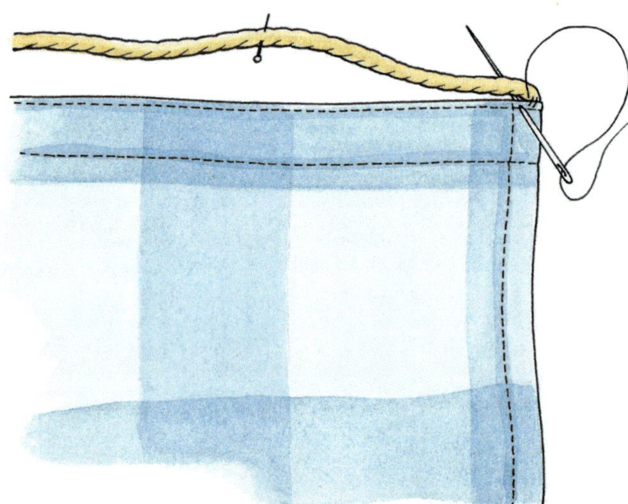

4 Lay the rope along the top edge and stitch the rope to the edge taking a diagonal stitch through the underside of the rope and a straight one back through the fabric. Stitch for 1.5 cm (⅝ in). Measure 15 cm (6 in) along the rope and mark with a pin.

5 Form the 15-cm (6-in) piece of rope into a loop. Stitch through the base of the loop a couple of times to secure.

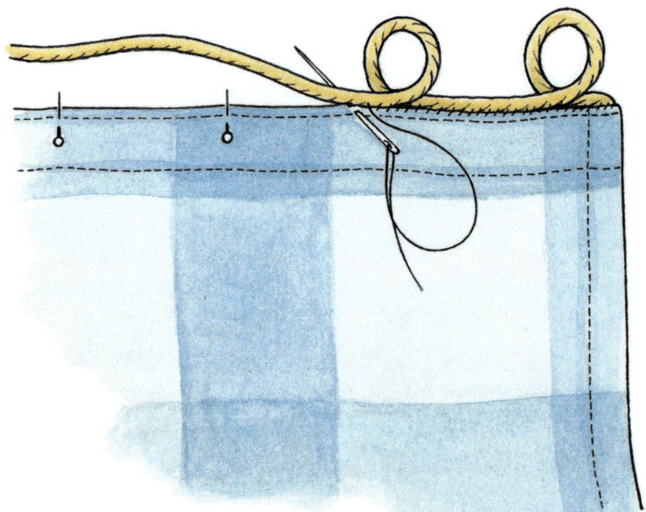

6 Stitch the rope along the top for 7.5 cm (3 in) then form and stitch another loop in the same way. Form as many loops as required then finish the end of the other side hem in the same way

7 Press an 8-cm (3¼-in) deep double hem to the wrong side across the lower edge of the curtain and machine stitch in place.

professional tip

If the rope or cord unravels at the ends, wrap adhesive tape tightly around the ends before cutting them then cut the rope at the centre of the tape. Leave the tape on the ends when they are tucked into the side hem. Alternatively, the ends could be dipped in fabric glue and allowed to dry before stitching the rope to the fabric.

variation on a theme...

country checks

Cool, country checks roped neatly to a fine pole make a great half curtain for a kitchen window. In this version, metal eyelets pierce the hem across the top of the curtain and the rope is simply threaded through and over the pole with the ends held by knots on the wrong side.

Make the curtain in the same way as the curtain on the previous page, then add eyelets centrally along the top hem, spacing them about 8–10 cm (3¼–4 in) apart. Knot one end of the rope then thread the rope through the eyelets and over the pole. Finish with another knot at the other end.

voile panels

These sheer curtains look great on French windows. They provide privacy while letting in the light and can also give a stylish look to wardrobes with glass panel doors. The panel can be made flat to give the effect of a blind fastened in place with a fine rod or tension wire threaded through the top casing. You could also thread a wire through the bottom casing for an ultra smooth finish.

MATERIALS
Fabric
Sewing thread

HANGING DEVICE
Rod or tension wire and metal screw eyes and hooks

SUITS...
Voile, georgette and other lightweight fabrics
Door, cupboard and wardrobe windows

CUTTING OUT

1.5 cm (⅝ in) seam allowances are included unless instructions state otherwise. Measure the required finished width and add on 4 cm (1½ in) for side hems. Measure the length and add on 6 cm (2¼ in) for hems. Cut out to these measurements.

METHOD

1 Press 1 cm (3/8 in) wide double hems along both side edges. Machine stitch in place.

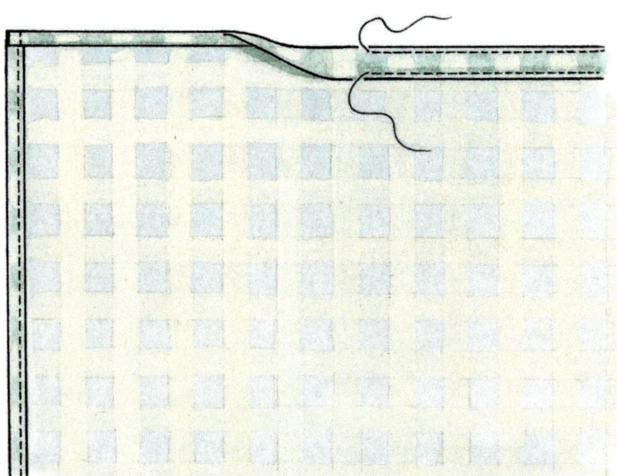

2 At the top and lower edges, press 1 cm (3/8 in) then another 2 cm (3/4 in) to the wrong side to make casings. Stitch in place along the both edges of the casing.

professional tip

Fix the top rod or tension wire in position above the glass and hang the curtain in place. Then thread the other rod or wire through the lower casing to establish the position for the lower fixings.

PRETTY SILK BOW TIE-BACK

For a pretty alternative, leave off the lower wire, pull back the panel to one side and tie back with a stylish silk bow.

variation on a theme... *gathered panels*

A fine georgette fabric in a soft shade of oyster pink is softly gathered to make these elegant door panels. The lightweight fabric will dress the door and provide more privacy without cutting down the available light. For the gathers allow twice the required finished panel width. These panels are made in the same way as the flat panels and are held taut at the top and bottom by plastic covered tension wires. These are held in place with small metal screw eyes, which hook onto small screw hook attached to the door.

eyelets and shower hooks

This innovative window treatment using chrome shower curtain hooks gives a really contemporary feel to any window. This design is ideal for use with thick cottons and linens and looks best if the fabric is plain rather than overly patterned. When fixing the eyelets, make sure they are positioned correctly at the top of the curtain to ensure that the shower hooks fit comfortably over the pole.

MATERIALS
Fabric
Sewing thread
Chrome eyelets size 14 mm
Chrome shower curtain hooks

HANGING DEVICE
Pole and finials

SUITS...
Cotton and linen fabrics
Flat and recess windows

CUTTING OUT

For the fabric width allow about twice the width for fullness. For the length add 20 cm (8 in) to the required finished length for hems.

METHOD

1 Press 1 cm (3/8 in) then 2 cm (3/4 in) to the wrong side along each side edge and machine stitch in place.

2 At the top edge, press 1 cm (3/8 in) then a 5-cm (2-in) hem to the wrong side and machine stitch in place.

> *professional tip*
>
> Before making eyelets on the curtain, make one or two test eyelets on a spare piece of fabric folded to give the same fabric layers on the curtain. The exact methods vary so practise following the manufacturer's instructions until you have perfected the technique. You may need to assist the hole cutting with a small pair of scissors. Work on a firm, solid surface that will not give or be marked when hammering the eyelet in place.

3 Position the eyelets so that there is one about 2.5 cm (1 in) in from either side edge and fix the others evenly between, spacing them about 12.5–15 cm (5–6 in) apart. Fix the eyelets so that the top of the eyelets are about 12 mm (1/2 in) down from the top edge. Follow the manufacturer's instructions to attach the eyelets.

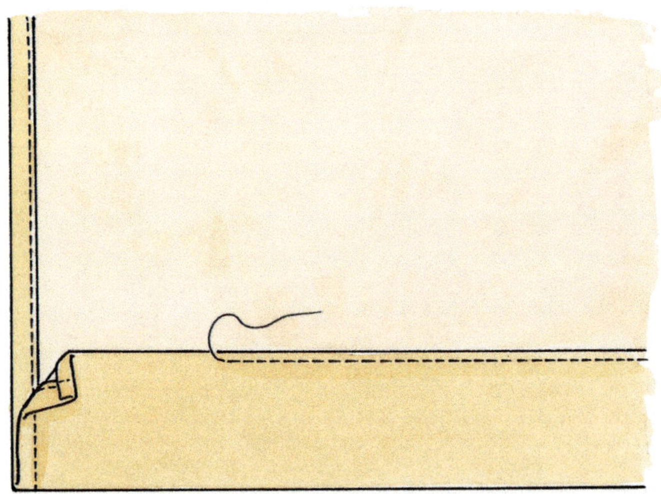

4 At the lower edge, press 1 cm (3/8 in) then a 12-cm (4 3/4-in) hem to the wrong side and machine stitch in place.

variation on a theme...
ready-made eyelets

A ready-embroidered broderie anglaise panel with ready-stitched eyelets at the top and a sweet scalloped edge at the base make a quick and easy half curtain for a kitchen or bathroom. The fabric comes ready-made by the metre though often in limited widths. All you need to do is press and stitch a double 1-cm (⅜-in) hem down each side edge, thread shower hooks through the stitched eyelets and the curtain is ready to hang.

café curtains

Café curtains that cover just the lower half of the window, are great in kitchens and bathrooms, to hide an ugly view or to provide privacy without cutting out the light. A smart checked linen tea towel with ribbon ties is great for a small kitchen window, or a pretty lace-trimmed tablecloth will give a softer look for a bathroom or bedroom.

MATERIALS
Tea towel
Matching sewing thread
Tape or ribbon 15 mm (5/8 in) wide
OR
Small lace-trimmed cloth
Flat-spring clips

HANGING DEVICE
Tension rod

SUITS...
Cotton and linen fabrics
Recess windows

MAKING UP

First work out how many ties are needed, spacing them about 10–12 cm (4–5 in) apart. Position the outer ties just inside the hems at either edge and the others evenly between, and mark the positions with pins.

1 Cut a 30-cm (12-in) length of tape or ribbon for each tie. Fold each tie in half and press in a crease at the fold. Lay the ties on the wrong side of the top hem on the tea towel at the positions marked so the crease is level with the hem. Pin and tack the ties in place and remove the pins.

2 Then machine stitch in place – each tie can be stitched separately though it is often quicker and neater to stitch one row right across the top edge.

LACE-TRIMMED CAFÉ CURTAIN

Fold over the top edge towards the front of the curtain to make it the right depth to fit between the pole and sill. Slip on a couple of clips and try on the pole to check the length. Then remove the clips and press in a crease along the fold. Attach the clips, placing one near each end and the others spaced evenly between and about 12 cm (5 in) apart.

sail curtains

This fun window treatment will obscure an overlooked view and is great for a themed child's room. The two straight-lined panels have eyelets in their lower corners and these simply hook back onto hooks on the wall to make the boldly effective sail curtains. The eyelets are just unhooked and allowed to drop to close the curtain.

MATERIALS
Fabric
Contrast fabric for lining
Sewing thread
2 chrome eyelets size 14 mm
2 chrome wall hooks

HANGING DEVICE
Velcro fastening 'stitch 'n' stick

SUITS...
Cotton and linen fabrics
Outside recess and flat windows

CUTTING OUT

Sail curtains are particularly effective when hung outside a window recess to make a little private area within. To do this, allow the curtain to overlap the wall by about 5 cm (2 in) all round.

1.5 cm (5/8 in) seam allowances are included unless instructions state otherwise. Measure the total area to be covered by the curtain and divide the width in half. Add 3 cm (1¼ in) to the length and the width, and cut two pieces to this size from the fabric and for the lining contrast fabric.

professional tip

Sail curtains look great with contrast patterned linings though the light can cause the pattern to show through the main fabric – check by holding the fabrics up to the light. To prevent this, place an interlining on the wrong side of the main fabric before stitching the pieces together. After stitching, trim the interlining seam allowance away next to the stitching.

METHOD

1 Place the fabric and contrast lining fabric together with the right sides facing and raw edges level. Stitch the two layers together around all edges leaving a 15-cm (6-in) gap on the side edge to turn through.

2 Trim the corners and turn the curtain right side out through the opening. Press the seam allowances to the inside along the edges of the openings and hand stitch the opening closed. Make both curtains in the same way.

3 Separate the two halves of the 'stitch 'n' stick' Velcro. Pin and tack the stitch half across just below the top edge of the curtain on the wrong side. Trim the ends to fit and machine stitch in place.

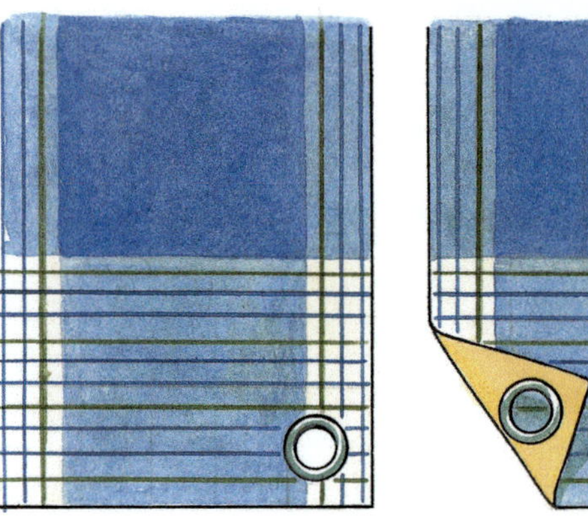

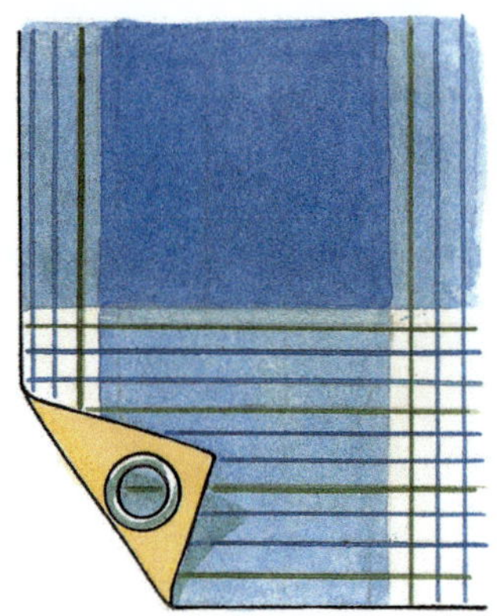

4 Fix an eyelet near the lower outer corners of each curtain following the manufacturer's instructions. Stick the other half of Velcro to the top of the window and attach the curtains. Finally, fix the hooks on the wall at the required position.

variation on a theme...

ring the changes

For a variation on how to rig your sail curtains, try attaching a curtain ring to the lead edge of the curtain, about a quarter of the way up from the bottom. Attach the ring to a hook on the wall so that the curtain edge zigzags down in a double fold to the base of the curtain.

casing top

This type of curtain has a casing at the top, which is made by folding the top edge over and stitching it down in a very similar way to a hem. This version gives a generous 6-cm (2¼-in) deep casing at the top to thread the pole through. This will give enough room for the curtain to slide smoothly along a medium-size pole. If you want the casing to fit more tightly, reduce the depth of the casing. For a wider wooden pole, increase the depth of the casing. Choose a light to medium fabric for this type of curtain, as a curtain with too much weight will drag on the pole and not pull easily.

MATERIALS
Fabric
Sewing thread

HANGING DEVICE
Pole and finials

SUITS...
Voile and other light- to medium-weight fabrics
Flat and recess windows

CUTTING OUT

Cut the length to the required finished length plus 18 cm (7 in). If you are using see-through fabric, add an extra 9 cm (3½ in) to the length. Cut or join to make up the required width, allowing 1½ to 2½ times the width for fullness plus 8 cm (3¼ in) for the side hems. The curtain shown has a 1½ fullness.

professional tip

On voile and other see-through fabrics, make a double hem, by folding the same amount to the wrong side twice, along the sides and lower edges to give a good, neat finish. In ordinary hems, where a small amount then a larger amount is folded to the wrong side, the different layers will show through the fabric and look unattractive.

METHOD

1 Press 1 cm (⅜ in) then a 3 cm (1¼ in) hem to the wrong side along each side edge and machine stitch in place. If using a see-through fabric, press and stitch a double 2 cm (¾ in) hem along each side edge.

2 Press 1 cm (⅜ in) then another 6 cm (2¼ in) to the wrong side across the top edge to make the casing and machine stitch in place along its lower edge.

3 Turn to the right side and machine stitch along the top edge of the casing near to the fold. This stitching will control the gathering and make it sit more smoothly on the pole.

4 At the lower edge press 1 cm (⅜ in) then a 10-cm (4-in) hem to the wrong side and stitch in place by hand or machine. Alternatively if you have allowed extra for see-through fabric press and stitch a double 10 cm (4 in) hem.

variation on a theme... double check

Pretty gingham fabric gives a country cottage feel to this variation on the casing curtain. A pair of small curtains, each tied with ribbon to make a tall X shapes, are hung on a tension pole to give a finishing touch to a small recessed window.

self-frill casing

This full curtain is gathered onto a pole or wire with a little fold of fabric projecting above to form a pretty self frill. It can be made to cover a whole window but it is particularly effective when used to cover just the lower half of a window to hide an ugly view or to provide privacy.

MATERIALS
Fabric
Sewing thread

HANGING DEVICE
Tension rod

SUITS...
Cotton, chambray, pique and chintz fabrics
Recess and flat windows

CUTTING OUT

1.5 cm (⅝ in) seam allowances are included unless instructions state otherwise. Measure the width across the tension rod (or wire) and the required length from the rod to the sill. Cut the curtain double the rod width by the required length plus 18 cm (7 in).

METHOD

1 Press a 1-cm (⅜-in) double hem to the wrong side down both side edges of the curtain and machine stitch in place.

2 Press 1 cm (⅜ in) to the wrong side across the top edge, then press 6 cm (2¼ in) over to the wrong side. Machine stitch along the pressed edge and again 3 cm (1¼ in) above it to form a casing.

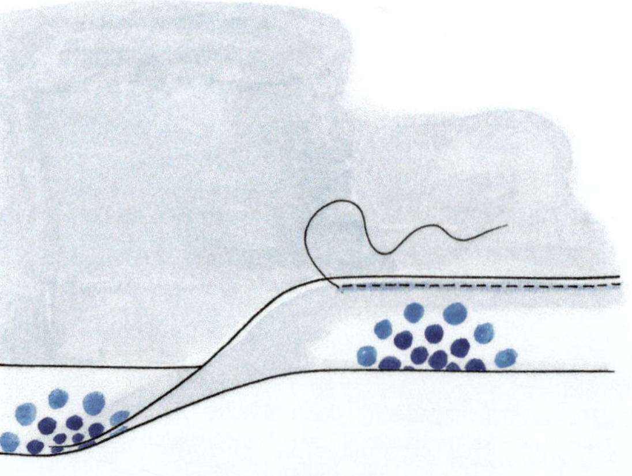

3 At the lower edge, press a double 4-cm (1½-in) hem to the wrong side and machine stitch in place.

deep self frill

This softly frilled curtain has a self-frill with a casing made in the same way as a standard self-frill (see pages 70–71), but here, the frill section in much deeper and when hung, the frill is pulled down to lie across the top of the curtain. This style works best on lightweight fabrics that look the same on both right and wrong sides.

MATERIALS
Fabric
Sewing thread

HANGING DEVICE
Tension rod

SUITS...
Cotton, chambray, pique and chintz fabrics
Recess and flat windows

CUTTING OUT

Measure the width across the tension rod or wire and cut the curtain double the rod width. To work out the required length, add twice the desired frill depth plus 1 cm (3⁄8 in) measured from the top of the pole to the finished length plus 8 cm (3 3⁄8 in) for the hem.

METHOD

1 Press a 1-cm (3⁄8-in) double hem to the wrong side down both side edges of the curtain and machine stitch in place.

2 Press 1 cm (3⁄8 in) to the wrong side across the top edge, then press the required depth of the frill over to the wrong side. Stitch along the first pressed edge then 3 cm (1 1⁄4 in) above it to form a casing.

3 Press 4 cm (1 1⁄2 in), then another 4 cm (1 1⁄2 in) to the wrong side along the lower edge to make a double hem. Machine stitch the hem in place.

gathered top

This softly-styled full curtain combines a gathered heading with pretty ribbon ties to fasten onto the curtain rings. The curtain is gathered up using curtain heading tape and the ties are slipped under the top edge of the tape before it is stitched in place. Choose ribbon or cotton tape for the ties according to the mood you want to create – ribbons will give a more opulent look while tapes will give more of a country feel.

MATERIALS
Fabric
Heading tape
Cotton tape or ribbon
Curtain rings

HANGING DEVICE
Pole and finials

SUITS...
Cotton, linen and silk fabrics
Flat and recess windows

CUTTING OUT

For the length, add 13 cm (5⅛ in) to the required finished length. For the width, allow plenty of fullness 2 to 2½ times the required finished width plus 8 cm (3¼ in) for side hems.

METHOD

1 Press 1 cm (⅜ in) then a 3 cm (1¼ in) hem to the wrong side along each side edge and machine stitch in place. If using a see-through fabric, press and stitch double 2-cm (¾-in) hems.

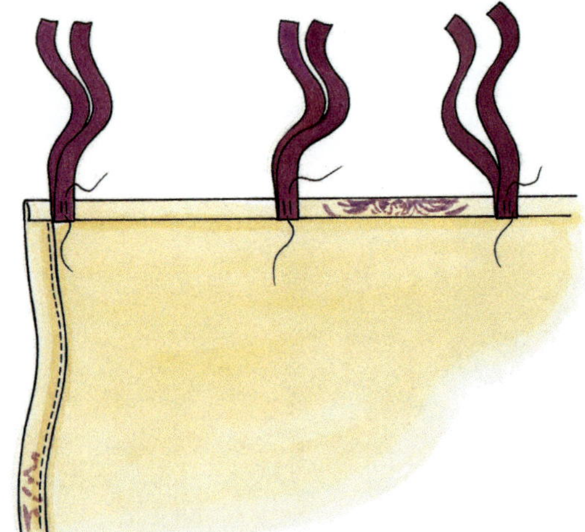

2 Press 2 cm (¾ in) to the wrong side across the top edge. Cut the tape or ribbon into 30–40-cm (12-16-in) lengths for each tie. Fold the tapes in half and press the crease. Place the tapes so the fold overlaps the top edges. Place one tape near each side edge and space the others evenly between so they will be spaced about 15 cm (6 in) apart when the heading is gathered. Pin and tack the tapes in place.

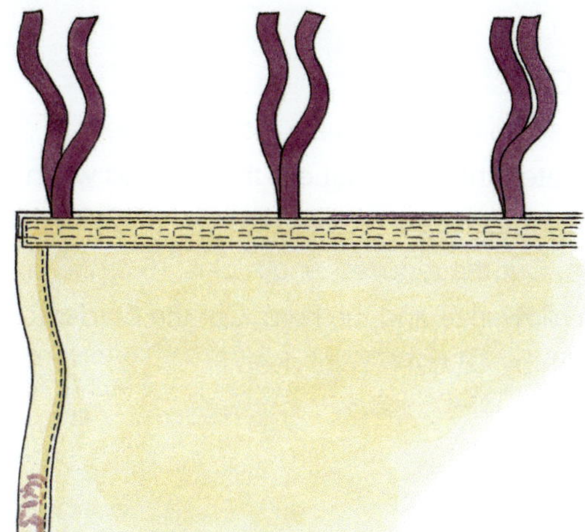

3 Turn under the ends of the heading tape for 2.5 cm (1 in) at each side edge level with the edge of the curtain. Stitch the heading tape in place up the side edge and across one edge of the tape and down the opposite side edge. Stitch the other edge in the same way so that the ends are stitched twice to ensure the cords are caught firmly in the stitching.

4 At the lower edge, press 1 cm (⅜ in) then a 10-cm (4-in) hem to the wrong side and hand or machine stitch in place. Pull up the heading tape to form tight gathers and fasten the cords neatly. Tie the tapes onto the curtain rings to hang the curtain.

eyelet top with contrast border

This dramatic floor-length curtain is made in a classic taupe-coloured fabric with a smart cream overcheck. The cream colour is picked out in the fabric for the wide border across the top edge and this is punctuated with bold chrome eyelets to thread onto the curtain rail. A purchased cream cord tie-back fastens onto a hook on the wall to complete the look. The curtain shown is made overlong so that it can puddle or bunch on the floor. If you would like your curtain to do this, you will need to add 15–20 cm (6–8 in) extra to the length to achieve this effect.

MATERIALS
Fabric
Contrast fabric for band to same width as curtain by 18 cm (7¼ in) deep
Sewing thread to match both fabrics
Chrome eyelets size 35 mm

HANGING DEVICE
Pole and finials

SUITS...
Cotton, polycotton and linen fabrics
Flat windows and French doors

CUTTING OUT

1.5 cm (⅝ in) seam allowances are included unless instructions state otherwise. Cut out the required width allowing extra for fullness if required plus 6 cm (2¼ in) for side hems. Cut the required length plus 15 cm (6 in) for the seam allowance and the hem. Cut the border to the same width by 18 cm (7¼ in) deep.

professional tip

To work out the length required for a tie-back, first hang the curtain and pull it back to the required position. Wrap a tape measure around the curtain at the chosen height for the tie back and hold the ends of the tape against the wall where the hook will be attached. Adjust to decide the length and position then note the length and mark the hook position on the wall.

METHOD

1 Press 1 cm (3/8 in) then another 2 cm (3/4 in) to the wrong side along each side edge and machine stitch in place.

2 Place the border across the top edge on the wrong side so the right side of the border faces the wrong side of the main fabric. Arrange so the top edges are level and the border projects evenly at both sides. Machine stitch in place across the top edge.

3 Trim the seam allowance to about 1 cm (3/8 in). Trim the projecting side edges of the borders 1 cm (3/8 in) outside the edge of the curtain. Press the seam upwards and 1 cm (3/8 in) to the wrong side around the other three sides of the border.

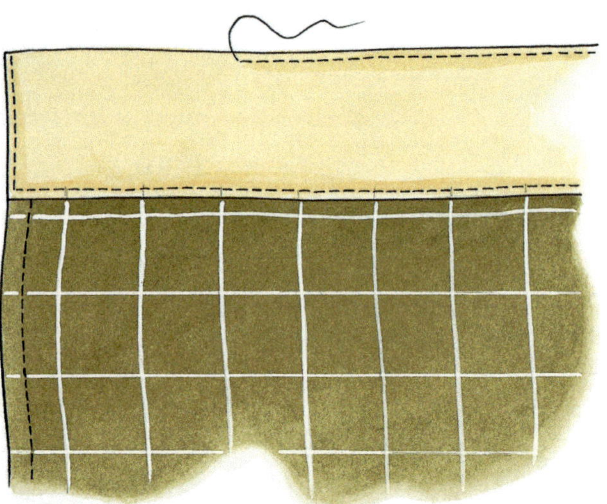

4 Fold the border over to the right side and press again. Stitch the border in place down each side and along the lower edge. Then topstitch along the top edge near to the fold.

5 Position the eyelets so that there is one near each side edge and fix the others evenly between, spacing them about 12.5–15 cm (5–6 in) apart. Attach the eyelets following the manufacturer's instructions.

6 At the lower edge press a 1.5 cm (5/8 in) then a 12 cm (4 3/4 in) hem to the wrong side and machine stitch or hand stitch in place.

variation on a theme...

double border eyelet top

The simple lines of eyelet curtains are shown to good effect with a top and bottom contrast border. For the lower border, subtract its depth and the hem allowance from the main curtain and add the hem allowance to the depth of the border. Add 1.5 cm (⅝ in) to the main fabric and the border for where they join. Stitch the lower border to the main fabric and make the top border narrower than in the main project.

ring top curtains

Hot pinks and vivid reds combine to make a sizzling set of ring-top curtains. The tops of the curtains are finished with simple plain hems to show the bold madras check fabric to best effect and curtain rings are stitched at intervals across the top edge. The rings thread directly onto the curtain pole to hang the curtains and a little extra fullness has been added to the width so the curtains drape softly between the rings when they are closed. Simple straight tie-backs are positioned high on the curtains to hold them back in dramatic drapes when the curtains are not closed. Curtain rings are also stitched to each end of the tie-backs to fasten onto wall hooks beside the window.

MATERIALS
Fabric
Lining (optional)
Curtain rings
Sewing thread
Curtain eyelet rings

HANGING DEVICE
Pole and finials

SUITS...
Silk, cotton and chintz fabrics
French doors and flat windows

CUTTING OUT

1.5 cm (⅝ in) seam allowances are included unless instructions state otherwise. These curtains can be made flat so when drawn they have no fullness, however, they usually look better with a little gentle fullness. For fullness allow 1 ⅓ to 1 ½ times the width of the area the curtains will cover, add 8 cm (3¼ in) to this for the side hems and 3 cm (1¼ in) for each join. For the length, add on 6.5 cm (2½ in) for the top hem and 15 cm (6 in) for the lower hem to the required length.

If the curtains are long, you may wish to make a deeper hem. Cut the lining 6.5 cm (2½ in) shorter than the curtain fabric at the top edge and 10 cm (4 in) narrower than the width.

METHOD

1 Join any fabric and lining widths if required with plain seams pressed open. Place the lining to the fabric with right sides facing and the top of the lining 6.5 cm (2½ in) below the top of the curtain fabric. Arrange the side edges level and stitch lining to fabric 1.5 cm (⅝ in) in from the raw edges finishing the stitching above the hem level.

2 Turn the curtain right side out. The narrower lining will pull the side edges of the curtain over to the wrong side for 2.5 cm (1 in). Arrange the hems evenly on both side edges and press in place.

3 Press 1.5 cm (⅝ in) then another 5 cm (2 in) over to the wrong side at the top edge of the curtain to form the top hem and stitch in place.

4 Decide on the spacing for the rings – between 12.5–15 cm (5–6 in) works well. To achieve regular intervals, divide the width of the curtain by the spacing to give the number of rings. Adjust the spacing so that the rings are evenly spaced with one near each side edge. Mark the position of the rings with pins.

5 Stitch the lower small curtain eyelet rings by hand to the back of the top edge of the curtain at the positions marked with pins. The lower edge of the rings can be stitched at the top edge so that they are visible, or lower down so that they are partly hidden by the curtain. Work small stitches side by side over the rings and through the back layer of the hem fabric.

6 Trim the lower edge of the lining 2 cm (¾ in) shorter than the edge of the curtain. Press a 7.5-cm (3-in) double hem to the wrong side of the curtain and stitch in place.

7 Make the lining hem in the same way so that it faces the curtain hem. Finish stitching the lining to the side hems by hand.

variation on a theme... *ribbon-tied rings*

A smart cream tablecloth will make a light and effective curtain for a small to medium size window. To make laundering easier, stitch ribbon ties to the top of the curtain and tie these to curtain rings to give a pretty heading which can be detached from the rings easily. First decide on the length for the ribbons, remembering you will need double the length hanging for each tie. Cut the ribbon to size, fold each in half and press the crease to mark it. Unfold the ribbon and position so that the crease is just below the top edge of the cloth. Stitch across the crease line. Stitch all the ribbons on and tie them to the rings.

tie top curtains

Simple but effective, tie top curtains are some of the easiest to make. We chose satin ribbon for the ties, which are neatly inserted between the curtain and a facing strip that finishes the top edge of the curtain. The curtains can be made to hang flat without any fullness when closed, in which case add 4 cm (1½ in) to the finished width for the hems. To add fullness to the closed curtains, cut them 1½ to 2 times wider than the finished width. With these informal curtains, it is best to use a whole or half fabric width whenever possible.

MATERIALS
Fabric
Sewing thread
1.5-cm (⅝-in) wide satin ribbon, 40 cm (15¾ in) for each tie

HANGING DEVICE
Pole and finials

SUITS...
Voile, cotton, chintz and chambray fabrics
Recess and flat windows, and French doors

CUTTING OUT

Cut the fabric to the required length plus 11 cm (4¼ in) by the required width for each curtain allowing for fullness plus 4 cm (1½ in) for side hems. Cut a 7-cm (2¾-in) deep facing strip the same width as the curtains.

professional tip

Dressing a curtain encourages it to hang in neat folds. Draw the curtain back and use your hands to form concertina folds across the width of the curtain in line with the folds at the top. Holding the pleats in place, tie around with a loose criss cross of fabric strips or tape. Repeat down the length of the curtain, leave to hang for two days then remove the strips.

METHOD

1 Press 1 cm (⅜ in) then another 1 cm (⅜ in) to the wrong side along edges of each curtain and machine stitch in place.

2 Cut a 40 cm (15¾ in) length of ribbon for each tie and press the ties in half. Mark the positions for the ties on the right side, one at each edge then others spaced evenly between, about 15 cm (6 in) apart. Pin and tack the ties in place so that the ties hang downwards and the fold is level with the top edge.

3 With right sides facing and top raw edges level, place the facing over the ties allowing it to project at each end. Stitch the facing in place 1 cm (⅜ in) down from the top edge.

4 Trim the side edges of the facing 1 cm (⅜ in) outside the curtain. Press the facing away from the curtain and press 1 cm (⅜ in) to the wrong side around the remaining raw edges. Press the facing over to the wrong side of the curtain and machine stitch in place along the side and lower edges. Then, if desired, machine stitch along the top edge on the right side.

5 Press 5 cm (2 in) then another 5 cm (2 in) to the wrong side across the lower edge and machine stitch in place.

variation on a theme...

country checks

Co-ordinating coloured ties will give a more casual country look to simple stripes and checks. Make the ties extra long, about 40–50 cm (15–20 in). Loop one end of the tie over the pole and use the other end of the tie to knot the two together at the top of the curtain so that the ends hang down in front of the curtain. Leave the ends straight or snip them across at a jaunty angle.

swags on poles

A simple length of fine linen or voile will drape beautifully over a pole to make an amazingly simple but effective window treatment. This type of treatment is ideal for decorative windows or windows which may not benefit from traditional curtains such as hallway windows. An asymmetrical drape will work well on most windows, but if you prefer it is simple adjust the lengths to make them even on both sides.

MATERIALS
Fabric
Sticky fixers

HANGING DEVICE
Pole and finials

SUITS...
Voile, lightweight linen and cotton fabrics
Flat and recess windows

MEASURING UP

To work out the length of fabric required, measure the length you wish the curtain to hang to at either side of the window. Measure the length of the pole area the swags will cover and add a third of the length again to allow for the swags to drape. Add these three measurements together to give the length required. If in doubt, round up the amount as swags need to be generous to look elegant. Allow the full fabric width so the selvedges can form the side edges of the swag.

METHOD

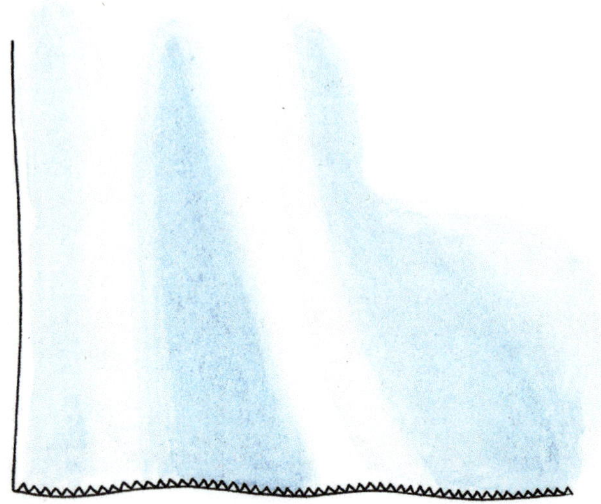

1 Stitch across fabric ends with a close zigzag stitch to stop the fabric fraying. This is all the making required.

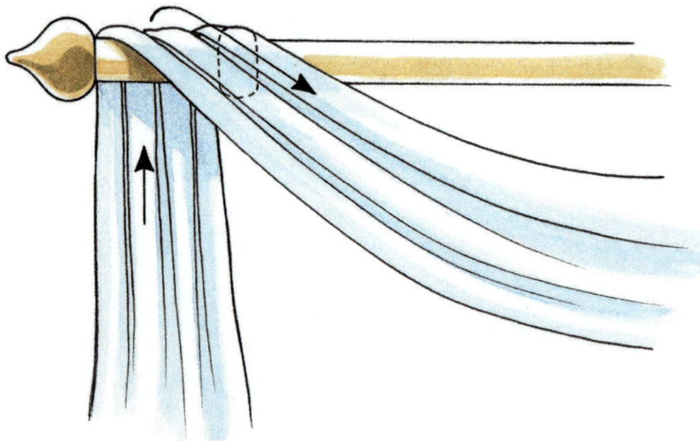

2 Arrange the drape over the pole first taking it up behind the pole at the left end outside the bracket bringing it over to the front of the pole.

3 At the centre of the window take the swag up behind the pole again and back over the front.

4 At the right hand end take the swag back behind the pole. Arrange the swags into pleasing drapes. If the fabric slips out of place fasten with sticky fixers between the fabric and pole at the back of the pole where they will not be visible.

variation on a theme...

fixed swag

For this swag variation, as well as draping, the fabric is also fixed in place on the top of the pole with a staple gun or drawing pins so the pole must be a wooden one. First, fix the centre section in place, folding the ends of the fabric into neat, draped pleats finishing on the top of the pole between the bracket and the end of the pole. Fasten in place temporarily with drawing pins then, when happy with the drape, staple gun in place. Lap the two separate end sections over the pole to cover the ends of the centre section. Arrange the lengths and pleats as desired then staple gun in place on the top of the pole.

double-layer swag

These can be made by simply using the whole width of the fabric so the selvedges form the side edges, or double side hems can be made, as shown, to give a more definite line to the edges. The double swags are made from two layers of contrasting fabrics so the front layer can be tied in a casual knot leaving the under layer to hang free.

MATERIALS
Fabric
Sewing thread

HANGING DEVICE
Pole and finials

SUITS...
Voile, lawn, fine cottons and fine silk fabrics
Flat windows

CUTTING OUT

Measure the required finished length from the top of the pole and add on 21 cm (8¼ in) for hems. For the width, allow about 1½ to 2 times the required width for fullness and 4 cm (1½ in) for side hems. Cut two pieces to these dimensions.

professional tip

As an alternative to knotting the outer layer, the single top layer could be draped and held back to one side on a decorative clasp or arm and boss. This could look particularly effective on a pair of curtains where they could be held back at each side. Or, for a handmade alternative, three strips of the fine fabric could be plaited together to make a fabric tie-back. Thread and stitch the plait onto a curtain ring at each end to attach to a hook on the wall.

METHOD

1 Press 1 cm (⅜ in) to the wrong side then another 1 cm (⅜ in) to the wrong side along both side edges to form double hems. Machine stitch in place. Repeat with the second layer.

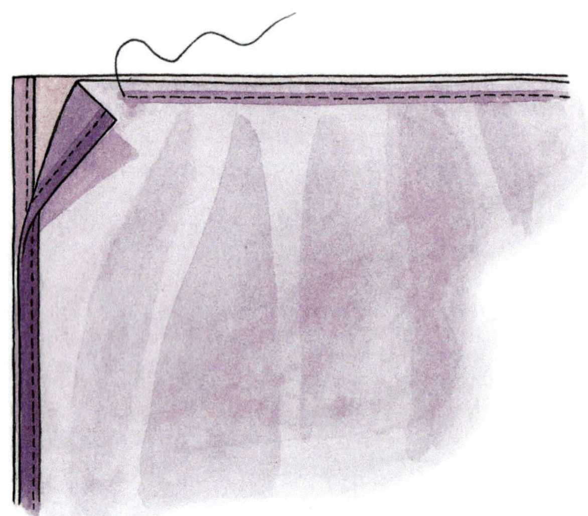

2 Arrange the top edges of the two pieces of fabric level with right side of the outer layer facing the wrong side of the under layer. Stitch together across the top edge 1 cm (⅜ in) in from the raw edges.

3 Press the top seam to one side first, then fold over so that the right side of the outer layer is on top and the seam is enclosed between the two layers of the curtain. Pin across 5–6 cm (2–2½ in) down from the top edge through both layers. Check the pole will fit in the casing. Tack if you prefer, or stitch along the line of the pins, removing them as you reach them.

4 Stitch a second row across near the top edge of the casing. This row can be stitched at the very top to make a wider casing or a little way level with the raw edges of the top seam to make a small self-frill.

5 Press 10 cm (4 in) then another 10 cm (4 in) to the wrong side along the two lower edges. Machine stitch the hems in place.

variation on a theme...

A silky gold outer layer blends with a deep violet under layer in this classy combination of colours and fabrics. A matching piece of violet-coloured fabric is used to form an unstructured tie-back to hold back the denser outer layer of the drape and reveal the finer violet voile under layer. This version is made with a taller self-frill at the top of the drape to stand up above the curtain pole. To allow for this, add 2.5–3 cm (1–1¼ in) to the length when cutting out. Add this amount to the depth of the first row of casing stitching and stitch the second row this amount down from the curtain top.

pointed panels

Grand pointed panels made from Jacobean-style embroidered fabric will dress a window with a hint of baronial splendour. The panels will not close like conventional curtains but they are a simple way to add style to an otherwise bare window. The flat panels are lined edge to edge on the wrong side and hang from simple clips, which hook onto the panels.

MATERIALS
Fabric
Lining fabric
Sewing thread

HANGING DEVICE
Pole and finials
Curtain rings
Clips with hooks

SUITS...
Wool, linen, velour and velvet fabrics
Flat windows and French doors

CUTTING OUT

Cut out the main fabric to the required length and width. The panel shown below is cut 40 cm (16 in) wide and 166 cm (65½ in) long including the 17-cm (6¾-in) long point. Cut out both the main fabric and the lining to the same dimensions.

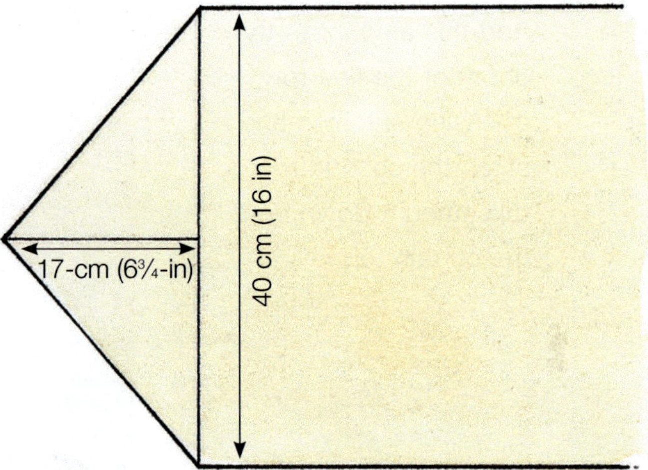

METHOD

1 Place the lining to the main fabric with the right sides facing and raw edges level. Stitch together around the outer edges 1.5 cm (⅝ in) in from the edge leaving a 15-cm (6-in) opening on the top edge to turn through.

2 Trim the corners: at the side points trim diagonally across the point outside the stitching. At the lower point trim diagonally outside the stitching then trim a further tiny wedge from either side to ensure a good point will be formed. Trim the top corners in the same way. Also trim the seams if they are bulky.

3 Turn the panel right side out through the opening on the top edge. Use a ruler or closed blunt scissors to push the points and corners out. Press the seams to the edge of the panel. Press the seam allowance to the inside across the opening and handstitch the opening closed.

4 Pinch the clip hooks to open them and fasten the clips onto the top edge one at either edge and one in the centre. If you have made a wide panel add more clips in between. Hook the clips onto the curtain rings to hang the panel.

variation on a theme...

tasselled panels

Narrow panels are also perfect for dressing small windows in a recess where there is no real need to close the curtains but a little dressing is needed to soften the space. The panel can be held back permanently with an elaborate rope tie-back to add to the decorative effect. This one features a splendid beaded tassel to complete the exotic look.

contrast borders

These stylish curtains have contrast borders to define the edges and add smart detail. The curtains can be as full or as flat as you like. We chose between 1¼ and 1½ times the fullness to add a little drape without making them too heavy. If you wish to line the curtains, cut and join any widths as required in the same way as for the main panel and tack the lining to the wrong side of the main panel before adding the borders.

MATERIALS
Main fabric
Contrast border fabric
Sewing thread
Optional lining
Curtain rings

HANGING DEVICE
Pole and finials

SUITS...
Cotton, polycotton, linen and chintz
Recess and flat windows, and French doors

CUTTING OUT

Cut out the main panels to the required finished width and length, joining any fabric widths as required. Cut the borders four times the required finished width – ours are 5-cm (2-in) wide finished. Cut the top and lower borders the same width as the main panel. Cut the side borders to the length of the main panel plus 3 cm (1¼ in) for seams.

professional tip

If you prefer a handstitched finish, prepare the border in the same way but press each side edge in an equal amount, leaving a gap so the edges don't quite meet at the centre. Stitch the border to the right side in the same way, then fold the other edge over to the wrong side level with the line of machine stitching. Slip hem in place taking the stitches through the back of the machine stitching.

METHOD

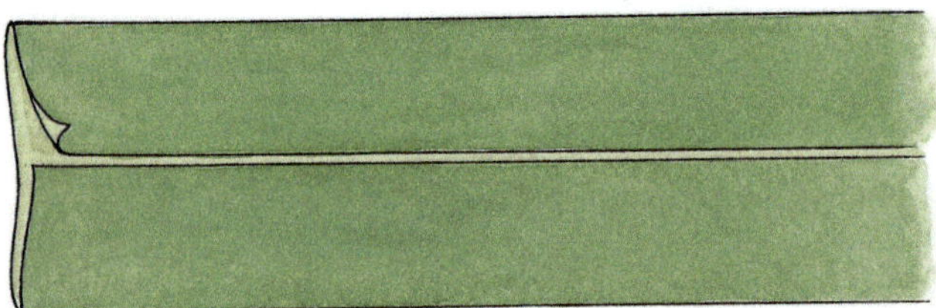

1 Press the borders in half then unfold and fold each side edge over to nearly meet at the centre but make one half of the border just slightly wider than the other. This slightly wider half will be the under layer half. Press in these creases.

2 Unfold the slightly narrower half of the top border and place it to the right side of the main panels with the raw edges level. Stitch in place along the pressed crease.

3 Fold the other half of the border over to the wrong side so the wider half overlaps the stitching slightly. Working from the right side, 'stitch in the ditch' by stitching along within the indentation of the previous seam to stitch the under layer. Stitch on the lower border in the same way.

4 Arrange the side borders so they project 1.5 cm (5/8 in) at the top and bottom. Stitch the first edge in the same way as the previous borders. Then fold the projecting ends to inside the border before stitching the second row.

5 Handstitch the short ends of the borders at the top and bottom. Finally, handstitch curtain rings inside the top edges to hang the curtain from the pole.

variation on a theme... fine fabric border

A delicate voile border will give a fine finishing touch to a pretty floral fabric curtain. Make the borders wider on larger curtains and narrower on smaller curtains to keep the proportion between the border and fabric well balanced.

tab top curtains

These simple unlined curtains hang from fabric tabs that are threaded onto a curtain pole. The curtains can be made to hang flat without any fullness when closed, in which case add 10 cm (4 in) to the finished width for hems. Or to add fullness to the closed curtains cut them 1½ to 2 times wider than the finished width. With the informal curtain, it is best to avoid joins whenever possible. The width and length of the tabs can be adjusted to suit the fabric and the size of the pole. Heavier fabrics and thicker poles require larger tabs than fine fabrics and thin poles. The tabs given have a finished width of 4 cm (1½ in) and are 10 cm (4 in) long.

MATERIALS
Fabric
Sewing thread

HANGING DEVICE
Pole and finials

SUITS...
Cotton, linen, silk and chintz fabrics
Recess and flat windows, and French doors

CUTTING OUT

1.5 cm (⅝ in) seam allowances are included unless instructions state otherwise. Measure the required curtain width and add the required amount for fullness plus 10 cm (4 in) for side hems. Measure the required length and add on 17.5 cm (7 in). Cut the tabs 11 cm (4¼ in) wide by 23 cm (9 in) long. Cut an 8-cm (3¼-in) deep facing to the same width as the curtain width plus 3 cm (1¼ in).

METHOD

1 Press 2.5 cm (1 in) then another 2.5-cm (1-in) hem to the wrong side down the side edges of the curtain and machine stitch in place.

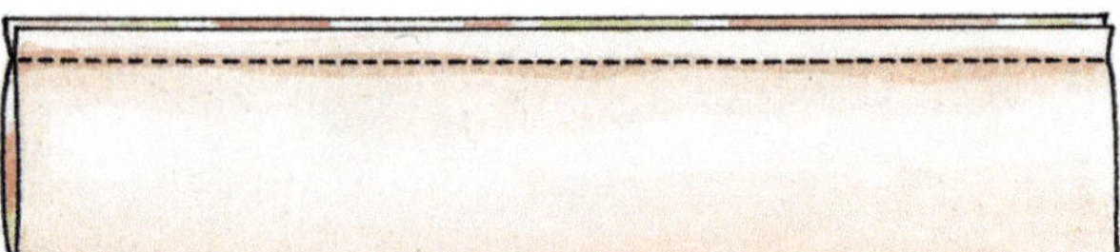

2 Fold the tabs in half lengthways, right sides facing, and stitch the two long raw edges together. Trim the seam and press it open. Turn the tabs right side out and press the seam to one edge. Topstitch along each long edge of the tabs if desired.

3 Fold each tab in half and place to the right side of the curtain. Place the raw edges level with the top edge of the curtain so that the tabs point downwards. Place a tab at each side edge and arrange the others so that they are spaced evenly, about 12.5–15 cm (5–6 in) apart. Tack the tabs in place.

4 With right sides together and the top raw edge level, place the facing across the top of the curtain on top of the tabs. Allow the facing to project for 1.5 cm (5⁄8 in) at either end. Machine stitch across the top edge.

5 Press the facing over to the wrong side. If the chosen fabric is see-through trim the fabric seam allowances to 1 cm (3⁄8 in). Press the seam allowance to the wrong side down the sides and across the lower edge of the facing. Machine stitch the facing to the curtain along the pressed edges. Topstitch across the top edge of the facing.

6 Press an 8-cm (3¼-in) deep double hem to the wrong side across the lower edge of the curtain and machine stitch in place.

variation on a theme... ribbon tabs

Make the tabs from simple strips of wide ribbon or cotton tape instead of making fabric tabs. Choose a colour to co-ordinate smartly with the fabric and simply substitute the ribbon or tape for the fabric tab when making up. An additional strip of ribbon or tape could also be stitched to the lead or lower edge of the curtain to co-ordinate the look.

triple pleat curtains

In this method, the curtains have hems made on the side edge of the fabric before the lining is attached. The lining is then hand stitched to the hems but left loose across the width from side edge to side edge. This gives a more lasting finish than the tube method used for the pencil pleat curtains but takes more time. The lower corners of the hems are also mitred for a finer finish. The hems at the sides and across the lower edge can be stitched by hand or machine. Hand stitching will give a finer finish while machine stitching will be quicker and give a more durable finish. For large curtains, it is worthwhile mastering the machined blind hem stitch.

MATERIALS

Fabric
Sewing thread
Lining
Triple pleat heading tape
Triple pleat hooks

HANGING DEVICE

Pole and finials

SUITS...

Cotton, linen and chintz fabrics
Recess, flat and bay windows, and French doors

CUTTING OUT

1.5 cm (5/8 in) seam allowances are included unless instructions state otherwise. To calculate fabric amount, allow 6 cm (2½ in) for each side hem and 3 cm (1¼ in) for each join. For the length, add on 4 cm (1½ in) for the top hem and 15 cm (6 in) for the lower hem to the required length. Cut the lining 4 cm (1½ in) shorter than the curtain fabric at the top edge and 12 cm (4¾ in) narrower than the width.

METHOD

1 Join any fabric and lining widths if required with plain seams pressed open. Press a 3-cm (1¼-in) wide double hem to the wrong side down the side edges of the curtain. Stitch in place by hand or machine.

2 Press 2 cm (¾ in) to the wrong side down the side edges of the lining. Place the lining to the wrong side of the curtain so the lining edges overlap the side hems by 1 cm (⅜ in) and the top of the lining is 4 cm (1½ in) down from the top of the curtain.

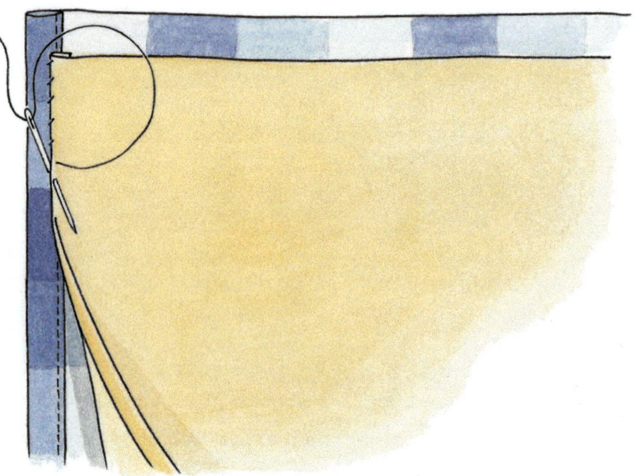

3 Hand stitch the lining to the side hems finishing the stitching about 5 cm (2 in) above the top of the lower hem. Trim the lining 3 cm (1¼ in) shorter than the fabric at the lower edge.

4 Press 4 cm (1½ in) over to the wrong side at the top edge of the curtain. Place the heading tape in position, aligning the top with the top of the curtain. Turn under the ends of the heading tape for 2.5 cm (1 in) at each side edge level with the edge of the curtain.

5 Stitch the heading tape in place up the side edge and across one long edge of the tape and down the opposite side edge. Stitch the other edge in the same way so the ends are stitched twice to ensure the cords are caught firmly in the stitching.

6 Press a double 7.5-cm (3-in) hem to the wrong side. Unfold the hem. At the side edge press the corner in at an angle on a line which begins at the side edge on the top fold and intersects the inner edge of the side hem at the lower fold.

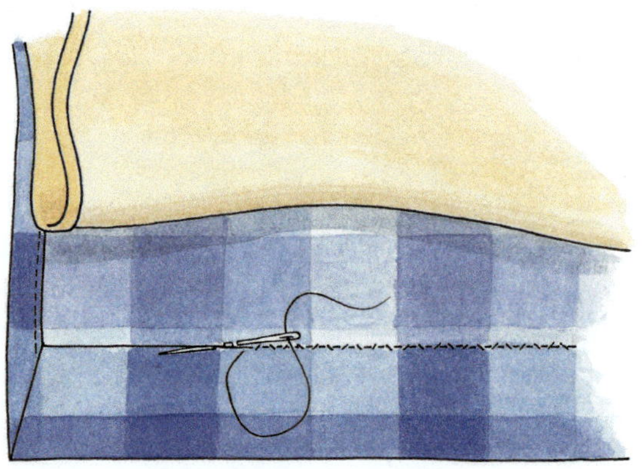

7 Refold the hem so it forms a neat mitre at the corner. Mitre the other corner in the same way. Hand stitch the mitres in place and stitch the hem in place by hand or machine.

8 Make a double hem on the lining the same depth as the curtain and machine stitch it in place. Complete stitching the side edges of the lining to the curtain side hems.

variation on a theme... border blues

Fresh cream and blues are combined in these double-border curtains to give a clean, modern twist to the traditional triple pleat heading style. Decide the depth of both borders in proportion to the length of the curtain. You will need to add the hem allowance plus 1.5 cm (⅝ in) for the joining seam to the lower border. From the main panel subtract the amount for the hem but add on 1.5 cm (⅝ in) for the seam. For the upper border, add 3 cm (1¼ in) to its depth for the two seams. First join any fabric widths if required then stitch the borders to the main panel and continue making up the curtain.

pencil pleat

The pencil pleat curtains are made by the tube lined method which is the easiest of the methods for making lined curtains. The lining is cut narrower than the fabric and the side edges of the lining and curtain are simply seamed together. The narrower lining pulls the fabric over to the wrong side to give the effect of a hem. However, these hems will have to be realigned and repressed each time the curtain is laundered. A pencil pleat heading tape is used to form the neat pleats at the top.

MATERIALS
Fabric
Sewing thread
Lining
Pencil pleat heading tape

HANGING DEVICE
Pole and finials

SUITS...
Cotton, linen and chintz fabrics
Recess, flat and bay windows, and French doors

CUTTING OUT

1.5 cm (5/8 in) seam allowances are included unless instructions state otherwise. To calculate fabric amount, allow 4 cm (1½ in) for each side hem and 3 cm (1¼ in) for each join. For the length, add on 4 cm (1½ in) for the top hem and 15 cm (6 in) for the lower hem to the required length. If the curtains are long you may wish to make a deeper hem. Cut the lining 4 cm (1½ in) shorter than the curtain fabric at the top edge and 10 cm (4 in) narrower than the width. If you wish to make the curtains overlong so that they bunch on the floor like those in the photograph, add 10–15 cm (4–6 in) to the curtain length.

METHOD

1 Join any fabric and lining widths if required with plain seams pressed open. Place the lining to the fabric with right sides facing and the top of the lining 4 cm (1½ in) below the top of the curtain fabric. Arrange the side edges level and stitch the lining to the fabric 1.5 cm (⅝ in) in from the raw edges finishing the stitching about 5 cm (2 in) above the hem level.

2 Turn the curtain right side out. The narrower lining will pull the side edges of the curtain over to the wrong side for 2.5 cm (1 in). Arrange the hems evenly on both side edges and press in place.

3 Press 4 cm (1½ in) over to the wrong side at the top edge of the curtain. Turn under the ends of the heading tape for 2.5 cm (1 in) at each side edge level with the edge of the curtain.

4 Stitch the heading tape in place up the side edge and across one edge of the tape and down the opposite side edge. Stitch the other edge in the same way so the ends are stitched twice to ensure the cords are caught firmly in the stitching.

5 Trim the lower edge of the lining 2 cm (¾ in) shorter than the edge of the curtains. Press a 7.5 cm (3 in) double hem to the wrong side of the curtain and machine stitch in place. Make the lining hem in the same way so that it faces the curtain hem.

6 Press the hems and arrange them to overlap neatly. Finish by stitching the lining to the side hems by hand.

variation on a theme...
lightweight option

Special lightweight pencil pleat heading tape is available for this light, bright and refreshingly airy option. It can be used on voiles, nets and other lightweight fabrics where the standard tape would look too dense. For this unlined option, omit any references to lining and stitch double 2-cm (¾-in) hems down each side edge of the curtain before stitching the heading tape on.

gallery

A collection of fine styles and great new looks to inspire the design of original window treatments – the gallery includes smart borders and cool colour schemes, contemporary and traditional finishes for stylish curtain tops, clever hanging devices and classy tie-backs and bosses to hold the drapes in place.

ABOVE Lightweight curtains drape back elegantly to make a frame for a day bed

LEFT Three toning borders give a strong contemporary look to an eyelet top curtain

LEFT Shades from the curtain fabric are chosen to colour furnishings and accessories

BELOW LEFT A deep hemline border and clever striped lead edge border add designer detail to plain curtains

BELOW RIGHT Rich, silk fabric and fine, smooth cotton are combined to give a delicate contrast of textures

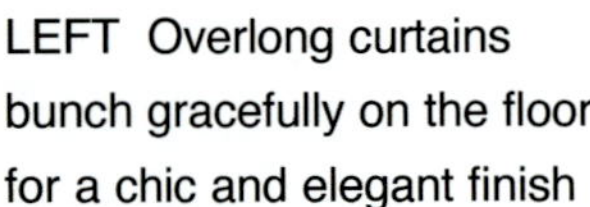

LEFT Overlong curtains bunch gracefully on the floor for a chic and elegant finish

BELOW Surface-stitched narrow ribbon trims add just a hint of colour to a minimalist scheme

LEFT High tiebacks make a witty frame of curtains closed at the top

BELOW Extra large eyelets thread directly onto a pole for a clean, uncluttered look

RIGHT Curtains stacked back beside the window enhance a light and airy feel

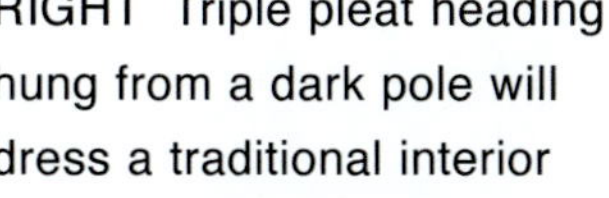

RIGHT Triple pleat heading hung from a dark pole will dress a traditional interior

RIGHT Multiple windows dressed lavishly make a major focal point

BELOW LEFT Novelty tiebacks chosen with care add a touch of élan and style

BELOW RIGHT A simple arm and boss make an elegant alternative to tiebacks for clean, uncluttered lines

LEFT Lovely lace panels with decorative finished edges add a charm all of their own

BELOW LEFT Brass clasps with fun, decorative heads are another neat alternative to tiebacks

BELOW RIGHT A gathered ribbon edging makes a pretty adornment around a painted arm and boss

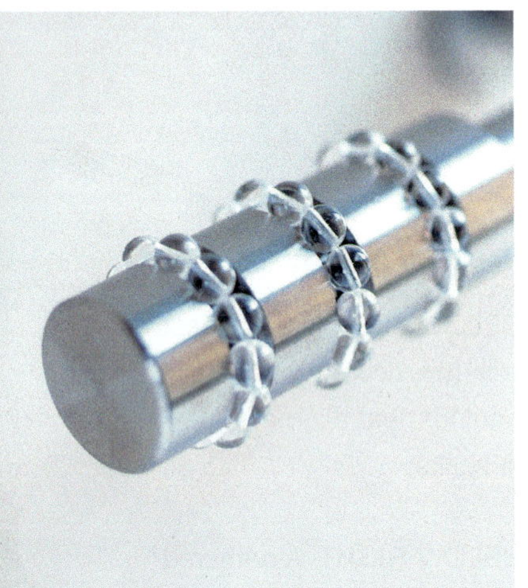

ABOVE Stylish finials add a smart finish to curtain poles

ABOVE Tabs and ties make great alternative hanging systems

ABOVE Clip-on curtain rings are speedy non-sew options

UNITED KINGDOM

Coats Crafts UK
PO Box 22
Lingfield Point
McMullen Road
Darlington
Co Durham DL1 1YQ
Tel: +44 (0)1325 394 237
Web: www.coatscrafts.co.uk
(sewing and needlecraft products)

Colly Brook Fine Furnishings
Colly Brook House
Knowbury
Ludlow SY8 3LN
Tel/Fax: +44 (0)1584 890315
Web: www.collybrook.co.uk
(mail order soft furnishings)

Franklin & Sons
13–15 St Botolph's Street
Colchester
Essex CO2 7DU
Tel: +44 (0)1206 563 955
(sewing machines)

Fred Aldous
37 Lever Street
Manchester M1 1LW
Tel: +44 (0)161 236 4224
Web: www.fredaldous.co.uk
(mail order craft supplier)

IKEA
Web: www.ikea.com

Janome UK Ltd
Janome Centre
Southside
Stockport
Cheshire SK6 2SP
Tel: +44 (0)161 666 6011
Web: www.janome.co.uk

John Lewis Partnership
Oxford Street
London W1A 1EX
Tel: +44 (0)20 7629 7711
Web: www.johnlewis.com
(fabrics, haberdashery)

Laura Ashley Ltd
27 Bagleys Lane
London SW6 2QA
Tel: +44 (0)871 9835 999
Web: www.lauraashley.com

MacCulloch and Wallis Ltd
25–26 Dering Street
London W16 0BH
Tel: +44 (0)20 7629 0311
Web: www.macculloch-wallis.co.uk
(fine fabrics and haberdashery)

Malabar
31–33 The South Bank Business Centre
Ponton Road
London SW8 5BL
Tel: +44 (0)20 7501 4200
Web: www.malabar.co.uk
(wholesale furnishing fabrics)

Perivale-Gutermann Ltd
Wadsworth Road
Greenford
Middlesex UB6 7JS
Tel: +44 (0)20 8998 5000
(threads and zips)

Prêt à Vivre
Shelton Lodge
Shelton
Nr Newark NG23 5JJ
Tel: + 44 (0)1949 851 178
Web: www.pretavivre.com
(curtain fabrics and hanging devices)

Selectus
The Uplands
Biddulph
Stoke on Trent ST8 7RH
Tel: +44 (0)1782 522 316
Web: www.selectus.co.uk
(fabrics and haberdashery)

Stitches
355 Warwick Road
Olton
Solihull
West Midlands B91 1BQ
Tel: +44 (0)121 706 1048
Web: www.needle-craft.com
(embroidery and sewing materials)

Velcro
Unit 1
Aston Way
Middlewich
Cheshire CU10 0HS
Tel: +44 (0)1606 738 806

Walcot House Ltd
Lyneham Heath Studios
Lyneham
Chipping Norton
Oxfordshire OX7 6QQ
Tel: +44 (0)1993 832940
Web: www.walcothouse.com

AUSTRALIA

Lincraft Stores
Adelaide:
Shop 3.01, Myer Centre
Rundle Mall
Adelaide SA 5000
Tel: +61 (0)8 8231 6611

Brisbane:
Shop 237, Myer Centre
Queen Street
Brisbane
Tel: +61 (0)7 3221 0064

Canberra:
Shop DO2/DO3, Canberra Centre
Bunda Street
Canberra ACT 2601
Tel: +61 (0)2 6257 4516

Melbourne:
Australia on Collins
Shop 320, 303 Lt. Collins Street
Melbourne VIC 3000
Tel: +61 (0)3 9650 1609

Perth:
St Martins Arcade
Hay Street
Perth WA 6000
Tel: +61 (0)8 9325 1211

Sydney:
Gallery Level, Imperial Arcade
Pitt Street
Sydney NSW 2000
Tel: +61 (0)2 9221 5111

Spotlight Stores
VIC +61 (0)3 9684 7477
TAS +61 (0)3 6234 6633
NSW +61 (0)2 9899 3611
QLD +61 (0)7 3878 5199
SA +61 (0)8 8410 8811
WA +61 (0)8 9374 0966
NT +61 (0)8 8948 2008

NEW ZEALAND

Embroidery and Patchwork Supplies
Private Bag 11199
600 Main Street
Palmerston North 5320
Tel: +64 (0)6 356 4793
Fax: +64 (0)6 355 4594
Toll free in New Zealand 0800 909 600
Web: www.needlecraft.co.nz

Hands Ashford NZ Ltd
5 Normans Road
Elmwood
Christchurch
Tel/Fax: +64 (0)3 355 9099
Email: hands.craft@clear.net.nz

Homeworks
First Floor Queens Arcade
Queen Street
Auckland Central
Tel: +64 (0)9 366 6119

Nancy's Embroidery
273 Tinakori Road
Thorndon
Wellington
Tel: +64 (0)4 473 404

Spotlight Stores
Whangarei +64 (0)9 430 7220
Wairau Park +64 (0)9 444 0220
Henderson +64 (0)9 836 0888
Panmure +64 (0)9 527 0915
Manukau City +64 (0)9 263 6760
Hamilton +64 (0)7 839 1793
Rotorua +64 (0)7 343 6901
New Plymouth +64 (0)6 757 3575
Gisborne +64 (0)6 863 0037
Hastings +64 (0)6 878 5223
Palmerston North +64 (0)6 357 6833
Porirua +64 (0)4 238 4055
Wellington +64 (0)4 472 5600
Christchurch +64 (0)3 377 6121
Dunedin +64 (0)3 477 1478
Web: www.spotlight.net.nz

The Embroiderer
140 Hinemoa Street
Birkenhead
Auckland
Tel: +64 (0)9 419 0900

SOUTH AFRICA

Crafty Supplies
Stadium on Main
Main Road
Claremont 7700
Tel: +27 (0)21 671 0286

Durbanville Needlecrafters
No. 1 44 Oxford
Oxford Street
Durbanville
Cape Town 7550
Tel: +27 (0)21 975 7361

Free State Embroidery
64 Harley Road
Oranjesig
Bloemfontein 9301
Tel: +27 (0)51 448 3872

Golden Stitches
14 Thrush Avenue
Strelitzia Garden Village
Randpark Ridge Ext 47
Johannesburg 2156
Tel/Fax: +27 (0)11 795 3281

Groote Kerk Arcade
39 Adderly Street
Cape Town 8000
Tel: +27 (0)21 461 6941

Habby Hyper
284 Ben Viljoen Street
Pretoria North 0182
Tel: +27 (0)12 546 3568

Nimble Fingers
Shop 222
Kloof Village Mall
Village Road
Kloof 3610
Tel: +27 (0)31 764 6283

Pied Piper
69 1st Avenue
Newton Park
Port Elizabeth 6001
Tel: +27 (0)41 365 1616

Simply Stitches
2 Topaz Street
Albenarle
Germiston
Johannesburg 1401
Tel: +27 (0)11 902 6997

Stitch 'n' Stuff
140 Lansdowne Road
Claremont
Durban 7700
Tel: +27 (0)21 674 4059

UNITED STATES

Ben Franklin Crafts
Web: www2.benfranklinstores.com
(fabrics, home decor, craft supplies and related merchandise)

Hancock Fabrics
One Fashion Way
Baldwyn, Mississippi 38824
Tel: +1 (877) 322 7427
Web: www.hancockfabrics.com
(fabrics, crafts supplies and related merchandise)

Hobby Lobby Stores Inc
7707 S W 44th Street
Oklahoma City, OK 73179
Tel: +1 (405) 745 1100
Web: www.hobbylobby.com
(fabrics, craft supplies and related merchandise)

Jo-Ann Stores Inc
5555 Darrow Road
Hudson, OH 44236
Tel: +1 (330) 656 2600
Web: www.joann.com
(fabrics, sewing and craft supplies, and related merchandise)

Rag Shop
111 Wagaraw Road
Hawthorne, NJ 07506
Tel: +1 (973) 423 1303
Web: www.ragshop.com
(fabrics, craft supplies and related merchandise)

ACKNOWLEDGEMENTS

The Publishers would like to thank the following for their generosity for providing all manner of fabrics, hanging devices, hooks and eyelets for the making of this book. Please refer to the Suppliers list on pages 125–126 for further information and contact details.

Colly Brook: 63 (wall hooks), 65 (wall hooks), 77 (eyelets)
Ikea: 57, 71, 93, 105, 113 (and for a selection of poles and finials)
Laura Ashley: 47, 75, 101, 107, 109
Malabar: 52, 77, 81, 85
Prêt à Vivre: 51, 63
Walcot House: 43 (b) (spiral rings), 61 (b) (twisted spring clips)

PICTURE CREDITS

John Lewis: 115
Laura Ashley: 2–3, 118 (r), 119 (br), 120 (t&bl), 121 (br), 122, 123 (t&bl)
Malabar: 40–41, 103, 116–117, 119 (t&bl), 123 (br), 124 (bc)
Prêt à Vivre: 79, 91, 111
The Pier: 99
Walcot House: 33, 118 (l), 120 (r), 121 (l&tr), 124 (except bc)

index

P

R

S

T

V

W

Z